On Influence and
Common Sense for
the 21st Century

On Influence and Common Sense for the 21st Century

Influence:
How to Exert It

Common Sense:
How to Exercise It

YORITOMO-TASHI

Published 2020 by Gildan Media LLC
aka G&D Media
www.GandDmedia.com

ON INFLUENCE AND COMMON SENSE FOR THE 21ST CENTURY. Copyright © JMW Group Inc. All rights exclusively licensed by JMW Group Inc., jmwgroup@jmwgroup.net.

No part of this book may be used, reproduced or transmitted in any manner whatsoever, by any means (electronic, photocopying, recording, or otherwise), without the prior written permission of the author, except in the case of brief quotations embodied in critical articles and reviews. No liability is assumed with respect to the use of the information contained within. Although every precaution has been taken, the author and publisher assume no liability for errors or omissions. Neither is any liability assumed for damages resulting from the use of the information contained herein.

Front cover design by David Rheinhardt of Pyrographx

Interior design by Meghan Day Healey of Story Horse, LLC

Library of Congress Cataloging-in-Publication Data is available upon request

ISBN: 978-1-7225-0336-9

10 9 8 7 6 5 4 3 2 1

CONTENTS

BOOK 1
Influence:
How to Exert It

7

BOOK 2
Common Sense:
How to Exercise It

143

BOOK 1
Influence: How to Exert It

Contents

Foreword to the Original Edition 11
Introduction by Editor of Original Edition 13
Note by Arthur R. Pell 17

Lesson I
By the Increase and Spread of Psychic Forces 19

Lesson II
By Persuasion 30

Lesson III
The Influence of the Eye 42

Lesson IV
Through Clearness of Speech 50

Lesson V
By Setting Good Example 58

CONTENTS

Lesson VI
By Psychic Influence   67

Lesson VII
By Decision   77

Lesson VIII
By Rational Ambition   87

Lesson IX
By Perseverance   99

Lesson X
By the Prestige Gained from Concentration   110

Lesson XI
By Confidence   124

Lesson XII
Acquisition of Dominating Power   134

Foreword to Original Edition

Yoritomo-Tashi, whose precepts are presented in this book, ranks as one of the three greatest statesmen that Japan has ever produced. He was her most illustrious and wise Shogun, and, as founder of the first Japanese dynasty of Shoguns, the reviser of the Empire's code of laws, and the organizer of military feudalism, he rescued his native land from the slough of demoralization into which it had sunk. In 1186 he established the seat of his government at Kamakura, where he organized an administrative body similar in its methods and operation to the metropolitan government. From what is known of his public career, it is evident that the great Shogun exercised a dominant influence over the minds of his people. To him the art of influencing others was the key to Success. The great philosopher believed that the spirit of the individual continuously exerts influence, even as the flower also exerts influence by spreading its fragrance in the air. But just as the blossom cannot tell whither its fragrance spreads, so none of us can say how far our influence may reach. To an anonymous writer we owe the thought that "Influence never dies." Every act, emotion, look, and word make it felt for good or evil, happiness or misery.

In the twelve lessons that Mr. B. Dangennes has drawn from the writings of Yoritomo-Tashi, and presents in this book, the manner in which Influence may be exerted and the means by which it may be exercised are considered. One lesson is devoted to the increase and expansion of psychic forces to awaken the dormant energies within us; another explains how influence may be exerted by persuasion and suggestion; a third shows the value of the fixed idea when supported by logical arguments; a fourth treats of the magnetic influence of the human eye and provides exercises for its development; a fifth deals with the power of good example; a sixth points to value of perseverance the achievement of great things by the utilization of spare moments; a seventh emphasizes the power of concentration, and provides exercises for its acquisition, and an eighth shows that by exchanging confidence one may exert a mighty influence that can benefit even those suffering from mental and physical ailments. "Confidence," says Yoritomo, "is the foundation of courage and the mainspring of action." How much our own Emerson believed in this aphorism he has told us—"Trust people and they will be true to you; treat them greatly and they will show themselves great." To confide in another, even though one be betrayed, is better than to conceal. Those who suspect evil are seeking in their neighbor for the very thing that they see in themselves, while those who exert a useful influence are people of strength and initiative who consecrate their energies to the achievement of that which is good.

Throughout the following pages the editor has provided suggestions, examples, and exercises as aids to the reader in the acquisition of this, the desirable art of knowing how to influence others in the world at large.

Introduction
by B. Dangennes, Editor of Original Edition

The success that has attended the publication of "Timidity Overcome," an earlier work by Yoritomo-Tashi, has encouraged me to print the precepts he developed on his methods of exerting influence.

The public can learn much from the old Shogun, whose doctrine, ringing with truth, is as applicable to the needs of our own day as in the time when it was first revealed.

Moreover, it is embellished with legends, gentle or austere, which suggest the sight of a smooth, grassy slope on which appear, here and there, scattered among rough oak trees, the rarest and most exquisite flowers.

Thus, it is with a deep and serious joy that I have again opened the manuscripts to transcribe in our own beautiful language the precepts and reflections of him who was at once a leader of men and a spiritual guide.

Again, little by little, I feel myself swayed by the charm already experienced; and the influence of these words, which seem to spring from the very beginning of time, and to have been diffused throughout the world, attract me and enthrall me with the doctrines of his philosophy in ever-increasing admiration.

Influence! that almost magical word, what things it suggests!

To influence others! What a marvelous gift, and what assured success to those of us that possess it!

We will know only by name the torments born of antipathy and of the loneliness of self-isolation from the rest of humankind.

The weaknesses of the will, the terrors that cause the rise of the phantom of agonizing doubt, will be strangers to us.

Both the spirit and the body will be under our command.

The griefs of life never will completely overwhelm us, for, having foreseen them, we will know how to mitigate them.

We will have the joy of seeing that people's hearts, under the influence of our word and example, will open to pure and noble sentiments.

The art of succeeding will become familiar to us, for we will know how to attract to ourselves voluntary collaborators.

In short, our power will set us apart as a being different from others, and, to use an ancient Japanese saying, filled with dominating power: "We will build our palaces on the bones of the timorous."

Little by little, the radiating action of this expanding will acts on me; why not try, through Yoritomo, to speak of this art, more magnificent than all others, since it renders contagious the cult of proselytism and shows us how to prevent it from becoming sterile?

To influence others! Is it not to play the part of creator, since it brings to life in all of our minds an idea, which without its aid never would have germinated?

Is it not to become a sort of providence, since good influence buries vice, the source of unhappiness and restlessness, to install instead perfect calm, the joy of living, and the security which always precedes happiness, or at least allows us to maintain ourselves in that state which most nearly approaches it.

With fervor, then, I have once more unfolded the writings of the philosopher, to transcribe the maxims and the luminous legends that make the study of his work so special and so attractive.

Although all truth is eternal, I trust that in this book, as in others that have preceded it, the reader will feel the undeniable and peculiarly genial attraction of the doctrine which the ancient Shogun exercises over the minds of those that know how to grasp and comprehend it.

Note
by Arthur R. Pell, Ph.D.

Why republish a book that was written close to one hundred years ago and based on the writings of a Japanese shogun who lived in the 12th century?

Sure, some of the concepts Yoritomo-Tashi promulgated may seem alien to the sophisticated minds of the 21st century, but his basic philosophy is to a great degree pertinent today.

B. Dangennes, a French editor and writer recognized this when he came across Yoritomo's writings in the early 20th century. He was impressed with his deep insight into the human soul and his direct style and brilliance in defining the various states of the soul. Unlike so many other philosophers—both in the past and currently—Yoritomo is neither prosaic nor depressing. Neither is he satisfied with merely pointing out an evil.

Instead he analyses its causes and suggest practical solutions.

In addition to this treatise on influence, Dangennes edited two other works by Yoritomo: *Common Sense: How to Exercise it* and *Timidity: How to Overcome it*.

The purpose of this updated revision is to clarify and strengthen the book without tampering with the content. To make Yoritomo's message more accessible to the modern reader, we have changed some of the language to replace archaic terminology and some of the examples that he used.

Just reading a book on influencing others will not help you become a more effective leader unless you apply what the author recommends. You may not agree with or be able to apply everything Yoritomo suggests, but many of his ideas can be put into practice today with the same effect as when used by the shogun in his lifetime.

Lesson I

By the Increase and Spread of Psychic Forces

"There is a country situated not far from the River Yet-Sin," said Yoritomo, "wherein certain villages are renowned for the curative property of the air.

"With the lightest breezes are diffused balsamic odors, which pour into weak lungs the restoring breath they pant for. At the coming of spring invalids gather there to install themselves temporarily in tiny houses which, seen from a distance, look like huge birds resting for an instant before retaking flight.

"My venerated master, Lang-Ho, took me one day to visit this privileged country, and, while admiring the beauty of the landscape, I could not refrain from actions that showed clearly my surprise.

"In the gardens that surround the small houses I see blooming the amaryllis, opening its gorgeous chalices, from which spring pollen laden pistils, looking like a woman's long eyelashes that have been made heavy with paint; in the flower-beds bloom roses, delicate or pronounced in odor; while large convolvuli climb the roofs and fall in jagged clusters.

"The fields extend monotonously in the distance; strips of land were planted with solid banks of chrysanthemums, whose bitter odor we could plainly detect.

"But above all other odors rose the balsamic fragrance of the resinous trees, vivifying and persistent. Yet, though I looked around carefully, I could perceive no sign of these trees, whose odor filled our lungs.

"Then my master looked at me and smiled:

"'I thought that you would be surprised,' said he; 'that is the common experience of those that visit this country for the first time; but how few among them are wise enough to draw a lesson from what they observed.'

"Pointing at a low hill, whose silvery verdure appeared to stand out like a luminous mass against a sky of tenderest blue, he continued:

"'Look! Behind that light screen of bushes is a grove composed of resinous trees. We cannot see them, but their beneficent influence diffuses itself throughout the surrounding country.

"'Do not neglect the lesson this teaches, my son! That little grove of regenerative power happily illustrates those people whose influence radiates upon and extends itself over those that approach them, in pouring out upon them the balm it distills.

"'Just as the light and frivolous birches hide the rough branches and roots whence proceed health and life, the art of influencing must learn how to surround itself with an aspect of amiability, and, in order to reach people's souls, it must abandon the idea that it must be composed merely of the rougher and more rugged virtues, so much extolled by many philosophers.

"'Influence must know how to enter the most thoughtless spirit, after the manner in which the balsamic odor penetrates these petty little houses, with their gardens filled with useless flowers.

"'Most invalids recoil at the mere notion of the boredom of living in the woods; but they come with pleasure to establish themselves among flowers, and yield unconsciously to the restoring influence, that radiates around them in the vivifying balsamic atoms.

"'With the coming winter they will depart. They will take up their old way of life, detaching themselves completely from that which has given them a new birth, so to speak; but they will bear within themselves this principle of new life, which has implanted itself without their will, and which will by slow degrees develop itself in the form of a desire to return.

"'Be not blind, my son, but receive seriously the lesson given to you by the immensity and simplicity of Nature.

"'As she influences the body, know that she influences souls also; and your earthly sojourn should contribute to the instruction of a strong and supple race, whose power will assert itself throughout the centuries.

"'People never really die who know how to assume sufficient empire over others to be able to trace lasting marks of their energy and power over the minds of those who, under their influence, bend their steps toward the highest.

"While he discoursed," Yoritomo continued, "I glanced around mechanically, and saw some of the inhabitants of these little pleasure houses. Some among them occupied themselves with light tasks of horticulture; others strolled about, chatting; the women, whom one could discern among the shadows of the terraces, were preparing tea with a cheerful rattle of cups; no one appeared to give a thought to the neighboring grove, yet every one felt its beneficent influence.

"An imperious and passionate desire arose within me to allow the expansion of the forces which energy, always working and always increasing, had put in my brain, that their powerful rays might penetrate weak souls and temper them for the bitter struggle of existence by reawakening in them a resolution toward good and a hatred of evil, simultaneously with the dauntless courage which is the keynote of all success based on noble ambitions."

A single word struck me in this last phrase of the Japanese philosopher.

He did not say, "to create," but to "re-awaken" in people's souls a resolution toward good and a hatred of evil.

It is this theory that our modern psychologists support so strongly; the plurality of types, which one may see verified in a single individual.

It is only in the simplest romances and the most naïve plays that individuals are good or bad all in the same way, without any variation.

On the contrary, it is easy to show that each individual is a prey, at a given moment, or in special circumstances, to contrary impulses, which show in him or her the presence of a double sensibility.

We will not speak of inclinations which correct themselves or grow weaker after reflection; for example, the sudden and unlooked-for prodigality of misers who fancy they may gain something by a show of liberality; the voluntary self-indulgence of people who know how prejudicial to them may be an appearance of excessive strictness or severity; or the temporary abstemiousness of gourmands who reserves their appetites for a feast.

Instinct more often takes the place of reason, in imposing on each person acts of contradictory sentiment, according to the time, the place, or the circumstances.

Our mind is only too often the field of evolution wherein are elaborated resolutions that are not dictated by an attentive and conscientious will.

Our modern way of speech calls such persons impulsive; following the bent of the idea that haunts them, they may be heroic or cowardly, proud or servile, kind or cruel; it is often impossible for the observer, as well as for themselves, to determine the exact quality, whether good or bad, that plays the chief part in the character of the normal person.

"There are those," Yoritomo continues, "who, dazzled by the fantastic dreams of a theoretic existence, recoil before the effort necessary to reestablish themselves in actual life and in stripping the rags of illusion from their chimera.

"All those, again, whom inertia holds ensnared in their vices will feel their hearts moved by an emotion leading toward light, and toward the practice of virtues indispensable to him who desires to face triumphantly the conflict of existence."

Note that the Shogun does not speak of "creating" the feeling that gives the impulse toward good; he wishes simply to awaken it, for he knows that it dwells within every heart.

If it does not manifest itself, it is because the psychic qualities necessary to its production cannot create successfully the initial impulse, which, fortified by the will and rendered more precise by concentration, will become efficacious in forming a habit.

But, in order to possess this gift in a way complete enough to exercise its beneficent influence over others, that it may be possible to suggest favorable thoughts and draw us back from the incline of baleful resolutions, it is indispensable that we should provide ourselves with that beneficent power which must radiate from ourselves, as heat rises from a glowing hearth.

What must one do to gain this power?

Listen again to the Shogun.

"We possess," said he, "innumerable forces that lie hidden within ourselves, though it would be easy to lead them, as the waters of a canal are conducted, to make them serve for the conquest of good, spiritual as well as corporeal.

"The existence of these forces can not be doubted; they abide in a latent state in some persons, and appear intermittently in others.

"It is the lack of domestication of these forces that causes the frequent and disconcerting plurality of the Ego.

"What can one think of people who today commit villainous crimes and who to-morrow, in the same circumstances, will perform acts of devotion?

"Thinkers have often deduced from this phenomenon the theory that in such people slumber different states of the soul, of which one, under the influence of a momentary emotion, surges up, to the exclusion of all others.

"These manifestations of the energies that are buried in the most profound depths of being are, unless they are concerned in our moral betterment, almost always regrettable because they are thoughtless, springing up incomplete and nearly always contrary to those designs which deliberate reason would help us to accomplish.

"It is wise to direct these efforts to a practical end, and not toward such realizations of which the accomplishment would give no virile satisfaction."

Apropos of this, Yoritomo related the following little legend:

"Once on a time lived a man who was in love with the queen of the clouds.

"His days were passed in contemplation of the skies; when the sun shone he was sad, but when clouds floated across the heavens like gray tatters lie delighted himself with fancying that he could behold his chimera.

"She was very capricious, and rarely assumed the same aspect twice. But from time to time he recognized her in some flocculent mass, whereupon his heart would swell with joy.

"At last he resolved to join her, and in order to do so he fancied he must build a monumental stairway that would reach to the sky. So he set himself to work, interrupting himself only to lose himself in the contemplation of his ideal.

"Years passed; his hair grew gray, his hands and knees trembled, but, faithful at his task, he continued painfully to add one step to another.

"At last a day came when the tottering builder, struggling in anguish against approaching death, attained his object; the stairway reached the clouds, from the midst of which his beloved leaned toward him. He climbed the last step and extended his lips to the longed-for apparition.

"But he received only the kiss of the rain which, dropping slowly, bore with it the form on which he had doted so many years.

"Returning to earth, the man wept.

"He wept for his lost youth, the beautiful years that had gone, and, above all, for his strength wasted in sterile efforts, when he might have put it to magnificent use."

May not this little legend be the origin of the story from which our modern writers have drawn the figure of Pierrot, the classic French clown, enamored of the moon?

Are there not many persons who pass their lives in building by slow stages a stairway that leads nowhere, and who do not perceive the fact until the work is finished?

The struggle for life becomes more and more arduous, and the power of our hidden faculties should expand in accordance with ever-growing necessities.

It is time, then, to awaken the forces that lie dormant within us.

"But," some one may object at this appeal, "evil forces as well as good will be aroused, and the combat between them will be so much the stronger because we ourselves must direct it."

The old Japanese philosopher had foreseen this objection, and he said quietly:

"Why fear to reanimate *all* the possibilities that lie dormant in our natures?

"Is it not desirable to cultivate all plants indiscriminately?

"There are those that are poisonous, true, yet even these are indispensable in the practice of medicine.

"Large doses of certain drugs cause death; but, administered wisely with the hand of a skillful physician, they bring relief and very often a complete cure.

"The same may be said of many forces that are evil only because they are not disciplined.

"There is still a danger to avoid; that of failing to discern those who can make us mistake for virtues the evil qualities that are only deceptive copies of virtues.

"Just as certain poisonous vegetables resemble those that are edible and wholesome, just as certain flowers have the form and color of those that are inoffensive, up to the point where only the initiated can detect the difference, there are failings, which, by their origin, resemble virtues of which they are really the direct opposite.

"But naturalists are not deceived; the poisonous plant is recognized by them in the midst of a hundred others, and if they gather it, it is only to extract its medicinal properties."

Philosophers, adept in researches touching suggestion, distinguish still more rapidly the "enemy" forces that disguise themselves under an appearance of false virtue.

"They will separate pride from vanity, perseverance from obstinacy, gentleness from weakness; and, strong, in this knowledge, they will know how to gather and to infuse into weak souls the infinitesimal dose necessary to produce the auxiliaries to success."

I observed that this word "success" occurred frequently in the remarks of the Japanese philosopher.

It was because it is the "Open Sesame" of the magic gates that lead to the domain so much desired.

Success! It is the fulfillment of one or of several desires, all converging toward one end.

It is the reason for living for those who wish to struggle for the conquest of Good—that Good which has a way of transforming itself and seems the farther away as soon as one has grasped it.

For wise people know the inanity of the word "perfection"; perfection cannot exist, since it can not be absolute and is always debatable, following the bent of differing tastes or the application of doctrines.

A thing, that seems to some persons the highest degree of *good*, will be criticized by others, whose convictions modify the ideal.

At this point Yoritomo, as he delighted to do, illustrated his words with a fable:

"A man once lived," said he, "who resolved to climb to the highest summit of a chain of mountains, so that no obstacle should hide from him the view of the universe.

"After countless fatigues, he climbed the peak which from below seemed to him higher than all the others; the ascent was rough, the road arduous and dangerous; but the man, possessed by his idea, felt neither the scorching sun which burned his face, nor the biting north wind on wintry nights.

"In order to avoid precipices and possible traps along the road, he walked with bent head, and did not raise it until the moment when his feet reached the lofty plateau, the object of his strenuous efforts.

"Alas! what disillusion was his! A granite wall, which clouds had heretofore hidden from his gaze, on looking up from below, rose before him, straight, rigid, impracticable, as it seemed to him.

"Impracticable? Not entirely so, but perilous, and above all mysterious, for the clouds that enveloped it hardly permitted him to discern the road that he must follow amid a thousand dangers.

"The man postponed the accomplishment of his desire. He descended into the valley again to wait for the dispersion of the clouds, so that he could choose his road by a clearer light.

"But that was not the real cause of his chagrin. The topmost peak was invisible from below, and he asked himself bitterly whether his great fatigue had not been caused by a mirage, after all.

"Should he begin another ascent? It was such hard work—it was better to wait! Now that he knew from which side he should climb to reach the summit, there was no need to worry about it. Besides, did a summit really exist? And even if it did, might he not encounter, after a weary climb, still another eminence, which he had not yet been able to discern?

"Days passed; the propitious moment did not present itself, and at last the man died in the valley, having lived a life interwoven with regrets and aspirations the more cruel because he well knew that he had not the energy sufficient to satisfy them.

"This often happens to those that assign to themselves nothing short of perfection as the end of their efforts.

"As soon as they imagine they have attained it, they try sadly to ascertain whether there is not something more left to conquer.

"Those among them who have become wise compel themselves simply to attain the highest, and soon acquire a passionate enthusiasm for their task, for their aim is not circumscribed but grand and infinite.

"One should pity those who believe themselves to have 'arrived' quite as much as those who despair of arriving. The former, thinking they have nothing more to combat, soon come to believe that there is nothing more worth conquering.

"Combat increases our energies, and the desire to live becomes more determined when one fears that one must die before the task has been accomplished."

"But," asked some one, "when should we enjoy the benefits of our continued efforts?" The answer was ready:

"From the perpetual pursuit of the highest springs a series of realizations, each of which gives us the joy and pride of conquest. Do traders cease to do business because they have just made a good bargain? While they appreciate the advantages gained in the long-pursued transaction, they will enter upon another into which they will throw themselves eagerly, and will even use the gains of the preceding bargain to make sure of negotiating the second.

"Thus we should use acquired forces, the advantages gained over ourselves, in the realization of another ideal, which, once attained, will allow us to pursue another of a form more nearly perfect.

"Those of us in whom moral strength does not grow and increase are very near decadence, and that means that we will enter on the road leading to shadows and death.

"Let us then turn resolutely toward the light; above all, let us increase our psychic forces, for they alone can give us that power that emanates from certain beings whose domination exercises itself beneficently over those that surround them.

"Just as when, in the heat of the sun, all grains and seeds sleeping in the earth's bosom sprout and rise in the form of plants to play their part in the universal fête of Nature, so under the power of influence always augmented and disciplined by noble deeds, the hearts of those near us will open to a desire for the best, conducive to the general aim of human kind—Happiness."

Lesson II
By Persuasion

How little we realize what a large part persuasion plays in our life. Clergy, teachers, lawyers, business managers, salespeople, parents—all are trying to persuade, to influence, to win over others to their way of thinking, to their principles, to accept their ideas.

Some people are so tactful, so sunny, so bright, cheerful, and attractive that they never have to force or even to request and entrance anywhere. The door is flung wide open and they are invited to enter, just as we invite beauty, loveliness and sunshine to enter our mind. Their very presence has a subtle influence in soothing and pleasing. They know how to persuade almost without uttering a word.

"Persuasion," Yoritomo taught us, "clothes itself in two very different forms; the one invades the soul like the invisible molecules of a soothing balm poured from a kindly hand, and gently infiltrates itself throughout our systems, communicating to us its virtues.

"The other may be compared to the terrible wind of the African deserts.

"If, from the first hour we feel its burning touch, we have not known how to avoid it by shutting ourselves closely within our dwelling, every crevice and opening of which has been sealed, nothing can escape its attacks.

"The imperceptible sand drifts little by little into all corners of the house, and even reaches all parts of the human body.

"However well protected we may be, it even penetrates closed lips and eyes, and soon this almost invisible thing dominates us and becomes our constant preoccupation.

"Evil persuasion is all the more dangerous because it knows how to clothe itself with the most attractive external attributes.

"That is what we meet in the guise of counselors whose words are always tempting, since they adopt the false appearance of solicitude.

"With earnest words and sympathetic smiles, these persons who almost always have nothing to do in life, try to spoil the lives of others, without having a suspicion of their unconscious crime.

"Usually these are the kind of persons that talk in apparent good faith about the freedom to live one's own life.

"They are those who seek the agreeable sensation of the moment, without giving a thought to the possible bitterness of tomorrow.

"They have to learn harsh lessons, for all that; often they are compelled to suffer for days and weeks in order to pay for one day of careless pleasure; but these days are either soon forgotten, or their lightness of character is such that they prefer to take the risk of drawing down on themselves serious troubles in the future than to make any effort in the present to avoid them."

Here Yoritomo, always ready with examples, related the following story:

"I once knew a young man, the son of one of my friends, who was afflicted with a certain lightness of judgment.

"He was not bad at heart, but his effeminacy and lack of strength of will made him an undesirable companion for such of his young friends whose souls were not sufficiently tempered by the practice of a continual appeal to dominating forces.

"One day he was calling on one of his friends, whose father occupied an important place in the senate, and who sent his son to the house of one of his colleagues to learn the result of a discussion in which he had not been able to take part. Apropos of a very important question, on which a favored future or a disgrace depended, he wished to know what a night session of the senate had determined.

"On the way, the son of the senator confided his apprehensions to his frivolous friend.

"To this young man these weighty matters seemed unimportant and childish, and he dwelt much on the bore it would be to allow this matter to spoil an evening in which both friends had promised themselves much pleasure.

"His reply filled the senator's son with consternation; the night session had taken place, and the most important affairs had been discussed, and the absent senator had been attacked with great bitterness by his adversaries.

"But the friend said, 'Since the *contretemps* is sure to bring trouble and spoil the pleasure we were looking forward to, why risk this trouble? We can tell your father that the session did not take place, and that all is going well!'

"The senator's son resisted; he would not dare lie to his father, he said. But his friend became more insinuating: 'It would not be a serious lie, and besides, one would have time to say that some one had misunderstood—in fact, are we quite sure that there had not been some misunderstanding?'

"In order to vanquish his friend's last hesitations, the young gentleman pretended to recall the whole interview, analyzing its details and inventing others. Meantime, he said, they would say that several persons had stopped them and questioned them; was it not to one of these that they had replied?

"He said so much in so persuasive a way that at last the senator's son deliberately told his father that the expected session had been postponed until the following day. Under the influence of this evil persuasion he felt not the slightest remorse in telling this falsehood, and passed a delightful evening.

"But alas! the next day must have been terrible!

"His father and his partisans could not be found at all in time to foil the scheme of his enemies; his disgrace was decided on, and the order to commit hara-kiri was sent to him.

"After he was dead, his effects were confiscated, and his son dragged out the miserable existence of the poor beings whom will and dignity do not console."

The old philosopher did not tell us whether the friend, the cause of all these disasters, sought to palliate them by coming to the aid of him whom he had ruined by his detestable counsel.

But it is probable that, feeling in this affair as those feel who are conscious of their contemptible conduct, he looked on indifferently at the misfortunes chargeable solely to his own lightness of character.

It is, in fact, a common trait with those who are conscious of their own inability to make the least effort to experience a wicked sort of pleasure in observing the failure of others.

Another variety of the agents of bad persuasion are those persons we call pessimists, whom Yoritomo describes thus:

"One should flee those who are created with life which makes one think only of the stupor of death.

"Their souls are always in the state where one finds the body in the tomb; every effort seems useless to them, or rather, they prefer to make a show of that indifference which makes the gestures necessary to obtain the accomplishments they pretend to despise.

"Despise them, indeed? Do they not feel, rather a malicious joy in demoralizing others?

"They like to consider humankind as fundamentally bad, and to declare that the slumber of the dead is the superior of all other pleasures.

"That is true only regarding those who, as we have said, pass through life as if they were already dead.

"They would be right, perhaps, if one heard only through pleasures of the gross, earthly joys of existence.

"But, for those that know how to see, the joy of living is in all things, and we can taste it, even in the midst of the greatest afflictions.

"Can the grief of mourning, cruel though it may be, prevent us from admiring the sunshine at the moment when it hangs the purple of the sunset in the sky before it sinks to sleep behind the quivering birch-trees?

"Can any grief, whatever it may be, prevent us from feeling a delicate emotion on hearing the sweet, strong voice of a boatman, whose song is lost in the distance when his light craft disappears in the golden mist of the great lakes.

"The joy of life throbs everywhere about us; it is in everything that surrounds us, and we should gather all our strength to cry out against those that preach pessimistic doctrine, for every life, sad though it may be, is worth living."

Do we not hear those that talk about the scourge of our day, neurasthenia—which often is only one of the commonest forms of egoism for those that are attacked by it—refuse not only to believe in the beautiful and the good, but they devote the last sparks of their fast-disappearing will to persuading others of the uselessness of everything.

Are they always sincere? Do they not do this in a sort of spite against those who are more expert in the art of living and who excite their envy by enjoying the blessings of life that their own moral weakness does not allow them to appreciate.

How much happier are those of whom Yoritomo says, "They accept joyfully the evil of living," and show it in their fervent adoration of everything that is beautiful and good.

"These," he added, "are the true priests of favorable persuasion.

"They know by the authority of their own conviction, how to give courage again to the weak and faith to the incredulous.

"By the virtue of persuasion, they banish from the invalid the pains which almost always hasten the apparition of imaginary sufferings.

"They know the right words to say to strengthen weak wills, and to give to those who suffer pain in reality the courage to support the ills which sympathy and solicitude made lighter.

"They are, in short, true healers.

"The persuasion toward health is the best of panaceas, for no one denies the influence of moral qualities on physical health.

"I once knew a man who, under the influence to one fixed idea, was about to die.

"He imagined that, while drinking the water of a stagnant pool, he had swallowed a serpent, minute at first, but which growing larger inside of his body, caused internal ravages of which he felt himself likely soon to die.

"His friends had told me of his singular case, telling me how anxious they were at seeing this so-called invalid wasting away day by day.

"I was curious to visit him; I found a real invalid, looking very ill, with features sunken, and hardly able to drag himself about. Pressing his chest, he told us that the serpent was devouring him.

"His friends laughed at him and seemed to think that I would join them in their mirth, but I judged the moral evil too serious to try to soothe him by trying to reason with him.

"Persuasion alone, based on a real or an imaginary proof, with the aid of suggestion, could save the man.

"Instead of laughing with the others, I pretended to believe that he was really ill, and asked him to tell me his story, to which I listened with the deepest attention.

"To his great astonishment, I sympathized with him in his trouble, and spoke of one of my friends, a famous healer, who would be happy to interest himself in the invalid and to try to save him.

"Two days later I returned, actually bringing with me a physician whom I had told of this strange mania, and who had promised me his assistance, for it was indispensable to have near me some one who could speak authoritatively in order to impress the mind of the invalid.

"He examined the patient carefully, prescribed certain medicines, and withdrew, without giving any words of positive hope.

"Then began my part, that of a psychologist.

"I pretended that I would tell him the absolute truth, however brutal it might seem. The doctor had discovered beyond all doubt the presence of the serpent; he had tried certain medication. Would it succeed? He dared not affirm it.

"Several days passed, with alternating fear and hope, which indications I noted carefully. Finally, one day the physician declared that he was about to make a decisive test, of which he had great hope of a favorable result.

"I had known so well how to be persuasive, and had understood so thoroughly how to surround the patient with the right occult influences, that he no longer rejected the idea of a possible cure; and when, after taking certain medicines that induced him to vomit freely, we showed him the serpent which he believed he had thrown up, our invalid found himself suddenly cured.

"After this, if he happened to feel again pain or discomfort of any kind, he attributed it to the ravages caused by the serpent, and, as the cause existed no more the evil soon disappeared.

"This case shows that one of the conditions of succeeding in the art of persuading is not to batter rudely at convictions that one wishes to uproot.

"This hardly requires an explanation; in order to persuade some one, it is necessary to merit his or her sympathy; now, one never gains the sympathy of those whose opinions he or she does not share.

"Hence, in order to persuade successfully, one must banish suspicion and know how to listen.

"One must not forget the profound egotism that characterizes all imaginary invalids; they are so full of themselves that their ills seem to them to acquire high importance.

"They can not admit then that the whole world is not interested in their aches and pains, and the importance they themselves attach to them is a subject of development for their malady.

"For it is incontestable that all moral emotion has an immediate repercussion on the physical state.

"To be able to persuade patients that they are cured is, in most cases, to free them from their malady; it is always infinitely attenuated, since it is to spare them moral uneasiness, which exacerbates their bodily ills."

But Yoritomo did not stop here with instructing us in the benefits of persuasion; he extended his remarks to the unfortunates who are assailed by the doubt even of happiness, and he encouraged them with this parable:

"A young lord was passing one day along the highroad when the sedan chair, on which he was being carried, was struck so roughly that it was broken to pieces. He looked at the ruins a moment, then he ordered his bearers to go in search of a new one, and sat down by the roadside to wait for them to bring it.

"A poor man passing by stopped and talked with him about the accident.

"'And what shall you do with these pieces?' he inquired.

"'Why, nothing,' the rich man replied; 'I shall leave them where they are.'

"'Then will you allow me to take them?'

"'Yes, since I don't want them.'

"The beggar then set himself to work; he readjusted the boards, washed the soiled spots on the hangings in the nearest brook, and did so much and so well that toward evening the sedan chair, although a little deteriorated, it is true, was solid and fit to use again.

"Just then the bearers returned. They had not been able to find anything but a chair so light and frail that, as soon as they tried it, they saw that it would not do.

"There the beggar intervened, and offered the chair he had just repaired.

"The young lord was glad to pay a large indemnity to have the use for several hours of a thing which in reality belonged to him.

"And that," adds the old philosopher, "is the experience of many persons who will not understand that a destroyed happiness may prove a kind of blessing, if one knows how to gather up the pieces.

"Instead of grieving over them and abandoning them by the wayside in order to wait for what may turn up, is it not better to do as the beggar did and to seek in the mishap a security which we should find it difficult to be sure of in the coordination of new events?

"It is on such occasions as this that the power of influence comes into play.

"In order to persuade people that it is easier for them to work at the construction (or reconstruction) of the happiness that is near them, psychic power is more necessary than it is in drawing them into hypothetic adventures.

"The fascination of beginning over again has attractions for not a few people and how many more rely on luck which they almost deify!

"When can they convince themselves that, for those who know the power of influence, which develops a steady will and a strong thought, luck is born chiefly of circumstances created by ourselves.

"Almost always we are the architects of our own fortunes; it is in working at them without respite that we may model them if not wholly according to our wish, at least in a way somewhat approaching it.

"It is by believing steadfastly that we shall attain the highest power, that we shall acquire the qualities that make us almost more than human, since they allow us to govern and subdue those by whom we are surrounded."

Might we not say that here Yoritomo presented the "superman" of Nietzsche, and do we not find in all those theories a commentary on the modern phrase of the power of mind over matter?

In what manner does this evolution produce itself and above all by what means can one obtain these quasi-miracles?

How does one make this effort to attain the desired end, and what qualities, occult or material are necessary to develop to attain this magnificent ambition to conquer the minds of others?

You can learn to be a persuasive person.

While it is true that some people have more natural capacity than others, it is also true that most people can, by training, acquire the skills needed to succeed.

Let's look at the one job where persuasiveness is a major element—salesmanship. Even if you are not selling a product or a service, but are selling your ideas to other people, you must think of yourself as a salesperson.

Whether you are selling a product or selling your boss to accept your ideas or persuading others to change their minds about a political issue, the steps of persuasion are the same.

The first step is to get the other person's attention—otherwise nothing you say will even be listened to. This is absolutely necessary before you can persuade anybody to do what you want done.

You can get attention by commenting about something you know will be of interest to the person to whom you are talking. It is not necessary to speak of trivial or extraneous matters to attract that person's attention. A direct question or comment on the situation involved is a good first step.

For example, if you wish to persuade colleagues to serve on a committee to evaluate a new piece of equipment, a comment about the frequent breakdown of current equipment would surely get their attention.

The next step is to get them to be thoroughly interested in your proposition. You must arouse their desire to embrace the idea you are proposing. Once this is accomplished, acceptance is almost certain. To do this you must appeal to their emotions—the heart rather than the head.

First, you must explore what the other persons really want. What is important to them?—what turns them on? To do this you must truly listen to what they say in answer to your questions. Listen carefully. Be prepared to pick up subtleties that can lead you to that person's real interest. Then by adapting your comments to fit into their desires, you are on the way to winning your point.

Persuasive power, the ability to win others over to our way of thinking, our way of looking at things, is not a simple quality. It is in reality made up of many admirable qualities, which have more to do with the heart than the head. It is the emotional traits of human nature, which enables one to win out in many instances where logical qualities would be of no avail.

The best and most successful teachers are not always the most learned, but those who get hold of the hearts of their pupils, whose kindness, personal interest, and sympathy qualities which, apart from scholarship, make the best teachers. These same qualities give all of us the basic ingredients of being persuasive people.

The bests sales people are those who look out for their customers' interests and only try to sell them what is to their advantage to buy. They will not work off a large bill of goods upon them, which they know in their hearts they should not buy.

The ability to make others think as you do is a tremendous power, and carries great responsibility. Remember that the people with whom you are dealing will be always on guard against any sort of deceit. They will be looking for evidences of insincerity. They have no intention of allowing themselves to be duped or lulled. *Be sincere!* Remember that there is no substitute for sincerity in any field.

Lesson III

The Influence Of The Eyes

Few persons escape the influence of the human eye. If its look is imperious, it subjugates; if it is tender, it moves; if it is sad it penetrates the heart with melancholy.

But this influence cannot be real and strong unless it is incited by the thought behind it, which maintains and fixes that look, in communicating to it the expression either terrible or favorable, persuasive or defiant, which alone can maintain the firmness and the perseverance of the active forces of our brain.

"Some persons," said Yoritomo, "possess naturally a fascinating eye; usually they are those who can maintain a steady gaze for a long time without blinking.

"But it is not sufficient to be able to throw a glance the persistence of which sometimes causes a passing discomfort, which almost always tends toward the subjection of spirits of the weaker sort.

"This look should be the projection of a thought in which the fixed form is definite enough so that its penetrative influence shall become efficacious."

"But," some one will say, "it is not always necessary to think, since several animals possess this power of fascination, like the snake, which holds a bird motionless under the power of its gaze, so that it never dreams of trying to use its wings to escape from its enemy.

"But if conscientious thought does not exist in the animal, it is nevertheless active in responding to instinct.

"In the brain of the serpent there is a blind but highly concentrated power that manifests itself by its eager desire to seize its prey, and this power, placed at the service of a forceful instinct, develops a compulsion that is sufficient to paralyze all desire to oppose it in the weakest creature."

But the serpent does not monopolize this privilege of fascination, if one may believe certain old French chronicles.

In the old book published by Rousseau in the seventeenth century, it is related that a toad shut up in a vase that he could not get out of found it difficult to endure the fascination of the human eye; at first, in evident uneasiness, it tried to escape; then, when convinced that that was impossible, it would return to its former position and stare at the person in its turn, and ended by dying of the effect of this peculiar force.

Is it necessary to lend strength to this story by adding that one day a toad, stronger or more irritable than the others, riveted its eyes so long upon a man's eyes that he actually felt the influence of the creature and swooned under the implacable fixity of its gaze?

I do not believe that such experiences have been officially established, but it is none the less interesting to conclude that if under the sway of an instinctive thought, the eye of an animal can acquire a rare power, the human eye, when animated by an active and reasonable thought, may be an important agent of influence and of suggestion.

"In order to convince your adversary," said the Japanese philosopher, "you must look him or her straight in the eyes.

"But it would be very stupid and unskillful to employ this method without discretion.

"Some would see in it only insolence, and their irritation would prevent them from feeling the full influence of the gaze; others would feel a certain uneasiness which would cause them to turn the eyes away before having submitted entirely to the gazer's influence, and might prevent them from renewing an interview with a person that had impressed them so unpleasantly.

"The best way to begin the use of the eye in influencing is to talk of subjects that will not arouse suspicion in the interlocutor.

"We should present ourselves in an easy and quiet manner and listen without showing any signs of impatience to whatever objections the person may make; some of these may not be lacking in accuracy, and it would be unwise to combat them.

"It is unnecessary to add that the least hastiness, which would displace the point of concentration of the thought, would be injurious, and might work serious harm to the success that we seek.

"Too great excess of modesty should be avoided, for the transmission of thought—and consequently of influence—is worked at our cost.

"Timidity is always an obstacle to the influence of the eye, which should, at the very first interchange of glances, look straight and frankly into the eyes of the interlocutor, at the top of the bridge of the nose.

"The first conflict once over, we should turn away our eyes carelessly; and should especially avoid the eyes of our opponent in the first minutes of conversation, before our own eyes have gained any hold on that person; we should in some way fix our gaze without allowing our opponent's eyes to gain a hold over our own.

"In short, if we wish to influence another by our look, we must take the greatest care not to let that person suspect our design, which would immediately put him or her on the defensive and render all our efforts vain.

"I once knew a young man named Yon-Li," added Yoritomo, "who went to call on a nobleman with the intention of serving as a mediator between him and one of his friends.

"In strict truth, I should say that the object of this proceeding was not wholly disinterested, since he wished to urge the nobleman to conclude a transaction that was injurious to his own interests.

"Besides, the friend had promised a round sum to Yon-Li if he should succeed in influencing this important personage to the point of accepting this solution.

"For a long time the young man had practiced exercises in the development of psychic influence, and he believed that he had arrived at the point when one is sure of himself.

"He entered and immediately threw on the nobleman a glance which the other thought rather singular; he tried to surmise the cause of a look which became almost aggressive in its expression of determination to dominate him.

"The nobleman was a man of strong will, who had for a long time exercised his powers of penetration.

"He had no great difficulty in discovering the motive that actuated the young Yon-Li, and he conceived the idea of fighting him with his own weapons.

"Taking care to avoid looking into the pupils of his visitor's eyes, he fixed him in the way which we have described, concentrating his gaze at the top of the bridge of the nose and strongly centering his thought on the idea of domination.

"The young amateur was not prepared to meet an attack more powerful than his own; his bold assurance faltered a little; under the influence of that penetrating look he blinked, lowered his eyelids, and gently turned away.

"He was vanquished, and it was with hesitation that he made his request. It was not entertained or even listened to, and he had besides the embarrassment of confessing, despite himself, the indelicate step which he had been ready to undertake."

Yoritomo added:

"The influence of the eye is undeniable; it is occult power set in vibration by the force of the thought; it is the result of the action of the forces that surround us, combined with our own vital force.

"One should not use these forces by chance. It is well to use them, especially, as arms, offensive or defensive, in the great battle won by wisdom and a knowledge of human nature."

But just as when he instructed us in the acquiring of energy, as well as when he taught us how to overcome timidity, Yoritomo did not content himself with uttering precepts; he told us the methods whereby we might acquire the precious gifts that he extolled.

"In order to attain that authority of the eye which is one of the first conditions in the study of acquiring mental dominance," said Yoritomo, "certain exercises are necessary:

"For example, it is well to lay a stick of bamboo across a sheet of paper, and then seat oneself at a few steps' distance and stare fixedly at the bamboo without allowing the eye to wander to the sheet of paper.

"One must use all his strength of will to avoid blinking.

"This exercise should begin with counting up to twenty, then to thirty, increasing the enumeration up to two hundred, which is enough.

"When one can perform this first exercise easily, it will be time to pass to another, a little more complicated.

"Having made a hole in the sheet of paper—taking great care to pierce it in such a way as to have the edges of the opening neat and clean-cut, rivet your fixed gaze on this aperture one, two, three minutes, longer if possible.

"It is well also to place yourself in front of a bright, smooth surface, preferably polished tin—lacking one of silver or gold—and to seek in it the reflection of your own eyes.

"Plunge your gaze into the inmost depths of your eyes; from the beginning this will be a good exercise in compelling the gaze of others to yield to your own.

"In this situation, turn the head from right to left, then from left to right, without losing sight of the reflection of your eyes.

"This strengthens the muscles of the eyes, and gives one's glance firmness and the desired power.

"Avoid blinking the eyes and lowering the eyelids, and practice meeting firmly the gaze of others."

But all these exercises would be in vain, if during the time of this contemplation, you do not know how to concentrate your mind on a single subject.

How much influence could you exercise over others if you do not know first how to master yourself?

Singleness of thought is indispensable during the development of the use of the eye; if it seems too difficult to keep it fixed on a single point, it would be well to avail oneself of certain means of suggestion, like the following:

"First, count up to ten with the simple idea of doing it slowly, and to allow the same space of time to elapse between the uttering of each number.

"Secondly, run through the fingers a string of about sixty beads, counting them in a low tone of voice, without losing sight of the point one has fixed on.

"You may count at first up to five or to ten; then increase the count, taking care to begin all over again if you find your attention has wandered, or that while pronouncing the numbers it has been diverted, if only for an instant, from the single thought that is the object of your purpose."

But this is not all; as soon as you have acquired the desired qualities in the cultivation of the power of the eye, you should begin to experiment with them, and regarding this here is what our philosopher counsels us:

"When you have mastered the use of the eye, and have learned how to concentrate the mind, try the ascendancy of your visual power on some person in the midst of a crowd.

"First, choose some one whose face indicates a character weaker than your own, and fix your gaze in the back of that person's neck, with a single thought, which shall invade that person's mind, haunting him or her with a desire to turn around.

"If your influence is already sufficiently formed, at the end of a certain time you will see that person begin to fidget, then to move his or her head slightly, as if to shake off an importunate thought; finally, your subject's hand will move to the spot on which your gaze has been fixed, then, without realizing the reason, he or she will turn around.

"This experiment may be made on all sorts of subjects, and it will always succeed on condition that you know how to envelop your subject in an intense mental current the action of which will combine itself with the power of your gaze.

"You can imagine, then, to what extent this faculty may be useful in the ordinary circumstances of life; it is the secret of those we call fascinating persons, whom no one can resist and who know how to obtain anything they desire by merely saying what pleasure it would give them to possess the desired object; for they know well that in concentrating the mind strongly on that for which they ask, the mind of their interlocutor, yielding to mental sway, abandons itself easily, especially if the domination of the eye increases this conviction by creating in that person a psychic state which compels submission to its power."

These precepts were those of that other tamer of spirits, Mohammad, who said:

"The effect of the human eye is indubitable. If there is anything in the world that can move more rapidly than fate, it is the glance of the eyes."

From this saying strong superstitions have arisen, against which the Shogun puts us on our guard:

"One of the reasons," says he, "that militate in favor of the cultivation of the influential use of the eye is the necessity of getting the better of a certain kind of persons who pretend to have inherited occult power from magicians.

"People gifted with strong wills have nothing to fear from these shameless liars; but sensitive and impulsive people, who do not know how to assert themselves and dominate others, become easy prey; and the suggestions of these wretches will soon lead them to dissipate their fortunes in answering their stupid requests."

"Besides," Yoritomo added, "those that would wish to use their occult influence to compel others to commit a wrong action would be soon punished by the loss of this influence, which develops itself gently only when actuated by beneficent thought; while they retract and end by becoming annihilated when the uppermost thought is of the kind of which may be said:

"Evil thoughts about others are rods with which we ourselves shall one day be beaten."

Lesson IV
Through Clearness Of Speech

The word is the most direct manifestation of the thought; hence it is one of the most important agents of Influence when it clothes itself with precision and clearness, indispensable in cooperating in creating conviction in the minds of one's hearers.

Were not the burning words of Peter the Hermit the sole cause of the rising of arms for the crusade to conquer the tomb of Jesus?

And was it not especially because that monk believed himself firmly to be moved by a divine will that he knew how to make his belief shared by thousands of men of all classes, poor or rich, who, under the influence of his words, all possessed only a single soul, impregnated with sentiments of heroic piety which urged them to dye the sands of Palestine with their blood?

What arguments had this monk found? Only three words, but powerful words, when one considers the mentality and the peculiar religiosity of that epoch: "God wishes it!"

"God wishes it!" These words were the first to declare to the ignorant masses Peter's all powerful influence. In the eyes of the vulgar, this man who transmitted to them thus the will of the Most High assumed in their eyes the proportions of a divine messenger, a sort of prophet in communication with the Master of Masters, who deigned to dictate to him His orders.

For others, it was to resume debates by an argument without reply; it was to excuse fatigues and privations, and an unknown death under a foreign sky. *God wished it!* How vain were all other speech after these three words, which bowed all heads under the powerful breath of divine domination, as wheat bends under the tempestuous winds!

Yoritomo speaks as a true sage, then, when he says:

"Leaders of souls should not forget this one thing: Too great wealth of words is hostile to conviction."

And, alluding to a Japanese proverb, which is very similar to one of our own well-known proverbs, he added:

"If speech is like jade, silence is like a diamond."

"Speech is like a diamond when it is the vibrating form of the concrete thought and when it presents itself in a quiet way, rendering its suggestions familiar and clear by the way in which the orator knows how to present them.

"Prolific speech is the medium of powerful thought—of that thought of which we should be master and not slaves.

"Speech is the seed, good or ill-omened, which, sown in irresolute natures, may produce either nettles or wheat.

"This may be also the 'fixed idea' that is supposed to be implanted in every weak brain.

"Suppose some one should chance to say to people, who are endowed with the power of initiative, but with a wavering will: 'You will be good, because goodness is the supreme end of life,' if the order is accompanied by the dominating look of which we have spoken and pronounced in a tone that will impress, there is no doubt that these influences will produce such a radiation as, in spite of themselves, would make them feel that they are under the influence of good emanating from themselves to converge toward other people.

"This may seem very obscure at first, but the brevity and precision of order will implant themselves little by little in the brain, of which the passive forces, always submissive to confused influence, will at a certain moment determine the active forces to emerge from the background where up to then they had lain hidden.

"But if one expresses this prophecy some day before a being afflicted with moral weakness: 'You will be a criminal,' the idea, originally repelled with horror, ends by sowing in the brain an idea first of the impossibility of the suggestion then, more frequently, evoked it becomes less monstrous. It commences with a smile of doubt, then it evolves to fear. By facing the eventuality of this prophesied crime, the specter which had been pursued so persistently a time will come, when carried away by anger or a violent passion this criminal act was committed, What previously that would certainly have been rejected was now replaced with a new idea which was perceived as the instrument predestined by fate.

"That is the reason why," added the Shogun, with infinite wisdom, "one cannot blame too much such parents as prophesy for their children terrible punishments for reprehensible acts which they can hardly help committing."

And he added:

"Those who, thinking to cure their children of faults more or less characteristic, repeat to them: 'You will die under the executioner's whip,' are sometimes the involuntary cause of this execution.

"To strengthen this idea of so lugubrious a fate for the little ones, they familiarize them with it, and dwell on its horrors.

"Then they compromise constantly their authority before their children, for they, seeing them the next day filled with kind feelings and expressing tenderness toward them, will not fail to regard lightly the terrible menace with which they were threatened.

"It might happen that they were struck by it, and that would be likely to be unlucky for their future, for, once implant this idea in their brains, they will not fail to wonder at the serenity of their parents, who can admit the possibility of so terrible a fate and yet go on living peacefully with the menace of such a future for their child.

"In every way, the authority of the heads of the family will find itself lessened, and the seed sown in the heart of the child by the imprudent prophecy can not fail to produce bad fruit.

"It will be so much the more dangerous if it should be resumed in a few words, those incisive words that draw mental pictures which take root in the brain.

"Long lectures have only a repressing effect on the spirit.

"One's listeners, endowed with will and discernment, very soon give up trying, under the avalanche of words that fall on their ears with the monotony of flakes of snow, to distinguish truths that are uttered in the confused mass of verbiage.

"On the contrary, they force themselves to turn these thoughts from this wordy chaos, in which the confusion equals the monotony.

"As for others, the laxity of their attention does not permit them to follow the same idea very long, and, all effort being painful to them, they will not long follow the orator's intricate mazes of thought.

"But those that know how to present their thought in a few phrases, in a way that impresses itself on their listeners, may easily become leaders of the masses.

"The first quality of the speakers who would be convincing should be to think deeply of what they wish to say.

"As soon as they know how to transform their thoughts into clear-cut images, the contours of which will not admit of any one's divining one line to be different from the line intended, they will be careful to project these thoughts into the minds of others under the form of lights and shades.

"We have already seen how the power of thought had the gift of influencing others, particularly when this, force is aided by the power of the eye; when these two ruling faculties are augmented by the power of spoken discourse, the listeners are conquered by the ideas that are presented to them.

"Those that will acquire these gifts will find that they can interest others and attach them to themselves; in a word can lead them by means of the influence that will assure them of mental empire over most of their contemporaries.

"It is necessary, also," the Shogun continued, "to base oneself on the theory that like attracts like, in the expansion of the sympathetic radiation which must converge toward great numbers to illumine the human soul.

"It has been remarked with what facility people follow noble impulses, heroic appeals, and generous outbursts.

"Speakers would be culpable, then, should they count on the inferior mental quality of their auditors in order to descend to their level.

"This is the fault of too many speakers who like to court less noble sides of the popular spirit.

"They give as a reason—I would almost say an excuse—that to address them in this way one is better listened to and more readily understood.

"This is a gross error. How many times have I uttered a noble thought in the midst of an assemblage of persons of mental mediocrity!

"As this thought was always expressed in language clear and exact, formed of words that all could comprehend, every time I have had the pleasure of seeing the multitude vibrate like a harp struck by an expert hand, and to feel for a moment that the souls of the roughest of peasants were elevated under the influence of my words which were adapted to the purest ideal.

"Is not this a kind of conquest for which those that devote themselves to the art of influencing should strive?

"It is by speech that one develops emotion, generator of noble gestures and of generous realizations.

"Speech is the distributor of the thoughts that surround us, of which the reiterated suggestions, after impregnating certain groups of cells in our brain, travel, by affinity, to haunt the same group of brain cells in other auditors.

"This is one reason why it is not well to dwell too long on the same subject, so that one can allow some rest to the weaker brains in an audience.

"Still, it is an undoubted fact that to jump from one subject to another, and to leave them only to attack them again, as is the custom of some speakers, is more fatiguing and less satisfactory, for minds wearied by this continual exercise end by ceasing to follow the flight of these fugitive thoughts; and, after waiting in vain for some repose in a discourse, they give up trying to follow the constant flight of a too soaring imagination.

"Another type to be dreaded are those devoted to idle chatter and gossip.

"One might, if he were greatly in earnest, correct them in this way: listen to their conversation, summarize it, and in ten minutes repeat to them all that it had taken them an hour to say; by 'all' one must understand merely the ideas and not the repetitions.

"But will they stand corrected? Will they not do as did a certain lord who, having seen his neighbor very ill, and having talked incessantly while visiting him, without letting the sick man get a word in edgewise, said, when leaving him: 'I will return to-morrow to learn how you are, for I fear I have tired you very much because I have done so much talking today.'

"Conciseness and clearness in speaking is thus a great force in the work of influencing, which is a noble task for one who undertakes it seriously.

"Moderation must be among the qualities whose aim is to second the action by the word in order to direct the focus of attention toward the principal thought which, excluding all accessory thoughts, should be imposed on the minds of the auditors by the speakers that wish to extend influence over them.

"Discretion is equally indispensable in forming influence by speech.

"From indiscretion to lying the step is short, and one should not forget this axiom that might well be written in characters of jade on leaves of purest gold:

"Lying is a homage which inferiority renders unconsciously to merit.

"Bands of precious metals should be hung on the walls of salons, replacing, in a way more comprehensible to all minds, the covered rose filled vases that ornament festal tables."

And Yoritomo reminded us of that ancient custom, which we believed peculiar to the Grecian sages, and which, it appears, was begun centuries ago among the philosophers of the Far East:

"Harpocrates, the god whom the ancient Greeks worshiped under the image of silence had presented to Eros, the God of Love a flower which, coming from his hands, represented the virtue which he was supposed to symbolize.

"This gift was made in order to encourage the wanton boy to guard the secrets of his mother Venus, for we know that Eros was always ready to reveal the secrets of those that were attacked by his flames.

"This act of the god was imitated first by the Grecian sages, then by the Japanese philosophers; and at all banquets appears a closed vase, the cover of which must not be lifted.

"This vase encloses the roses, whose perfume filters through the interstices of the vessel, letting one guess what flowers are within.

"It was a custom to ask the guests to let nothing transpire regarding the discussions that took place in these gatherings.

"Later the custom became general and was followed among ordinary people, when the closed and flower-filled vase was a constant warning to the guests to use discretion, and not to allow to escape outside anything that might have been said under the influence of wine.

"Our modern humor has immortalized this custom in the form of a figure of speech that is on everybody's tongue, but of which few persons know the origin: people often say of one who tells secrets: 'He has uncovered the rose jar!'"

The etymology of this figure is known to few, but, however that may be, we are grateful to Yoritomo for recalling it to us by connecting it with one of the lessons he has taught us, which, disguised in the form of a parable, fix them in our minds in so attractive a fashion that we do not forget them as soon as we have heard them.

Lesson V
By Setting Good Example

We read in a Japanese story that once man set out in pursuit of a rose. He sought it a long time, but nothing seemed to him to be that flower, which he knew only by hearsay, that praised its incomparable perfume and the beauty of its multiplex corolla.

"He saw the admirable amaryllis, balancing on flexible stems their odoriferous chalices, whose tender tints were touched with brown spots, that seemed like the tears of night.

"He had inhaled—quite surprised to find them without perfume—the breath of the proud peonies which bloomed near by, looking like a sort of burning bush.

"The fragrant stalactites of the acacias had breathed upon him their balmy odor.

"He had paused before carnations, which, crimson in their green chalices, looked like the throats of warriors, bursting out of their armor.

"The sumptuous mourning of the black lily also had attracted him; but none of these flowers were, nor could be, the rose, and he was almost in despair when he saw, quite near him, alight on a bush a butterfly of the most dazzling colors, and a delightful aroma seemed to be diffused from it, while its wings quivered like the petals of a flower shaken in the wind.

"Greatly moved, the man approached it, saying:

"'Beautiful creature, glowing with colors so brilliant and exhaling a perfume so sweet, can it be that you are the rose?'

"'No,' said the butterfly, 'I am not the rose, but I live near the rose; I love the refuge of her flowery arches and branches. I come to sleep in the hollows of her corollas, and sip the sweet perfume of her flowers.

"'That is the reason why I have become so thoroughly impregnated with her odor as to deceive you.'"

This little fable may serve as a preface to anything one might say or write on the force of example.

Our most frequent associations are never indifferent to our mentality, and we always submit, voluntarily or unconsciously, to the ascendancy of those that surround us, unless we have sufficient influence over their minds to compel them to submit themselves to us.

Then the thought, projected into an enveloping center by a superior influence, is received by brains of weaker caliber, which register it mechanically, in order to reproduce it on similar occasions.

Our popular modern philosophy has put this maxim into a proverb:

"Tell me who are your associates and I will tell you what you are."

It is explained also by Baron Charles Du Potet, a nineteenth century exponent of magnetism, in his "Magnetic Therapeutics."

"There are certain persons," he said, "who when near you, seem to draw something from you, to pump you, to absorb your force and your life; a species of vampire, without knowing it, they live at your expense.

"When near them, in the sphere of their activity, one feels an uneasiness, a constraint which is caused by their pernicious actions and determines in us an indefinable feeling.

"You are moved by a desire to escape and to go far away from them; but these people have quite the opposite tendency; they come nearer and nearer to you, press close to you, seem fairly to wish to join themselves to you, to draw from you that which is necessary to their lives.

"Other persons, on the contrary, bear with them life and health.

"Wherever they go, they seem to radiate joy and sunshine.

"You observe that their conversation pleases and that people seek them out. One likes to touch their hands, to lean on their arm; something soothing which charms and magnetizes you, quite unconsciously, seems to emanate from them.

"One easily adopts their point of view on things in general, and their opinions, without knowing why; and one sees them go away with sincere regret."

In short, above all things regarding psychic influence, we must not forget that "the strongest reason is always the best."

Unfortunately, the strongest is not always that which is worth the most; a regrettable contagion follows from the person who suffers the ascendancy of the other.

"Or again," the old Shogun explained, "the reciprocal influence which individuals exercise on one another is the cause of many evils difficult to conjure.

"That, if we may believe tradition, is the reason why the sages of old created so-called mutual admiration societies, to which only those of undisputed merit were admitted.

"In the numerous reunions, whatever might be the apparent reason for them, a low mentality evinced itself, and the general quality of thought became inferior, to such a degree that the most elevated mind felt the difficulty of escaping the contagion of the surrounding mediocrity.

"The only influence of orators might be to transmute souls momentarily by substituting for mean and niggardly thoughts a current of broad, generous ideas, from which would spring an enthusiasm real but almost always ephemeral, for at the moment of realization particular interests, narrow views, and the fear of responsibility will give back to each one of their auditors the mind that belongs to him or her, which a profound study of the attainment of the highest and best alone could transform slowly and definitively.

"However, certain such circles do exist which are composed of persons of absolutely pure aspirations, all communicant toward a noble end, in a collective thought, the waves of which are voluntarily directed toward a single accomplishment.

From these reunions of the best minds emanates a current of influence the value of which is considerable, since emulation, the offspring of example, is found in these circles where, each one developing, in a sense, from the same principle, concentrates his or her faculties on the search for the best in all that is good.

"But it is very difficult to maintain these gatherings under the unique direction of the original generous spirit. To find people who will ignore questions of temporary supremacy and of particular interests, and that know how to repress petty antipathies and hatreds, possibly more or less justifiable, in order to open the heart to the creation of an ideal—this is almost to expect the impossible.

"Is it, indeed, necessary to ask it? Is it well to suppress ambition in a person's heart? Does not such a leveling tend to destroy the seed of individual responsibility, a cognizance of which leads to the most noble conquests?"

While admiring the scruples of the Shogun, we could only regret that happy time when the ancient sages gathered with no other object than to talk of beauty in the heart of nature, in wonderful gardens in the midst of vegetation luxuriant and restful, with the blue heavens as their sole canopy.

But our modern civilization has other necessities, which find expression in a care, sometimes exaggerated, regarding subjection to the order of the hour: "Time is money"; it is necessary, then, that the time of the reunions should be limited, and that the place be carefully chosen, large enough to contain the public, which rarely would wish to assemble out of doors, lest the fine weather might change into a driving rainstorm.

It is of no use regretting things that cannot be changed; and it is wiser to listen to Yoritomo:

"I once knew a man who spent large sums in entertaining several Buddhist priests, who celebrated the cult by lighting an enormous quantity of lanterns, and by giving themselves up to various ruinous practices.

"I said to this man: 'It would be better to burn a single lamp before the statue of Buddha at his own home, and to invite all the priests who lead a useless existence in the temple to bear to the people the good word and to set them a good example.

"'Put together all the money which every year you would give to this sterile cult of Buddhism, divide it into as many sums as you would distribute to each of your priests in ordering them to distribute it among their poor as they teach them of the blessings derived in the name of Buddha.

"'Thus, glorified by example, the cult that you desire to honor would spread itself the more, since kind and charitable words would inevitably be connected with it in the minds of the unfortunates whom it had helped.'"

"The ability of certain actors," Yoritomo continued, "may be an influence, excellent or detestable, following the quality of the examples which they offer to the people.

"On the stage, an actor who has the gift of filling his very soul with the personage he represents can, at his will, sow the seeds of joy or terror, of admiration or desire for the beautiful in the minds of the spectators.

"That is the reason why we can not too strongly censure such plays as show a narrow or a vulgar mentality behind them.

"It is very wrong to impress the multitude with reproductions of criminal or reprehensible actions.

"While it is true that there are certain lower functions of our human nature that are common to every one, but which we mutually conceal, both from sight and by name, there are certain moral defects, certain ugly actions, a manifestation of which it would be very wrong to present to the eyes of the public.

"Do not the acts of generosity, of magnanimous impulses, and of heroic sacrifices offer a field wide enough so that it is not necessary to reproduce plays of sentiments and actions that are likely to be harmful?

"The influence of example is considerable, and it is a culpable thing not to circumscribe it to the representation of noble actions worthy of being imitated.

"It may be objected that in all plays in which a criminal is represented, malefactors are always punished for their misdeeds, sometimes in a way so terrible that the example can not fail to be of benefit as a warning to those that might be tempted to imitate them.

"That is an error common to those who occupy themselves with the study of psychology only in a superficial way.

"Among an audience capable of being influenced by these detestable examples, there are sure to be a few who will fancy themselves much cleverer than the criminals whose stories are being acted before them, and these will say to themselves: 'The crime was well-planned; and, if the perpetrators were taken, it is because they were clumsy.'

"For many, these reflections are theoretical, and they have no desire to imitate them. But what matters that? The evil seed has been sewn in them and, under the influence of an unworthy sentiment, hatred, calculation, or cupidity, it may develop into a fixed desire for dishonest conquest, of which the pictured crime was the origin.

"For those who are already tainted, the influence of such representations as we are considering would be even more vicious; for them the stage would be a practical school of vice, combined with astuteness and safeguarded from punishment by a thousand means which the actions of the players may suggest.

"One may say the same thing of books, though they are more dangerous for the erudite than for persons whose knowledge is more limited."

Alas! the Shogun knew nothing about compulsory education, nor of the thousands of cheap books, which propagate the taste for trying one's luck in the convincing tone of showing one how to make a fortune.

But it would be wrong to include the spirit of a book, which deplores all progress, which we praise highly. We should, however, emphasize very clearly the fact that too wide an education is often a two-edged weapon.

In some cultures, particularly in areas where many people do not read themselves, teachers, preachers or others in the community may read books, articles or essays to groups. Such readings should be on subjects at once lofty and interesting; but the result on the auditors when they are alone may be indifferent or beneficial, according to the mental qualities of the readers.

The reader should, above all things, be inspired with the principal contents of the preceding chapters, particularly those on the influence of the eye and thought-transference. To maintain dominance over the audience, the reader should look up from the book from time to time to maintain eye contact with them.

At the same time the ideas expressed should be backed by so powerful a thought from the reader that the thought-waves shall determine the mental current and act with the force of electricity."

Let us not forget also that personal influence radiates more certainly when it manifests itself under the form of altruism, charity, and kindness.

"Is it not a frequent thing," said the old Japanese, "to see a crowd hesitate, divided between a feeling of recrimination and one of approbation, and then suddenly turn toward conciliation, because one among them, on whom the situation and the influence of others had its effect, has openly declared agreement with those who favor conciliation?

"One of the greatest obstacles to the doing of good actions," he added, "is the timidity based on the fear of responsibility, which haunts mediocre minds.

"It is toward these that those who would wield the power of domination should turn their attention. It is sufficient to impose on these timorous souls the resolution to perform the task that they themselves desire to see accomplished, and to set them the example of their achievements.

"Their vacillating will strengthen itself by the moral support which they will be certain to feel, and their anxiety about the opinion of others will be soothed by the example of those whom they recognize as their superiors, and whose superiority they are glad to acknowledge.

"Example is the excuse behind which hasten to hide those whose ill-regulated thoughts cannot cooperate in defensive discernment.

"It is these, then, whose minds are strengthened by renewed practices of wise reflection, used in the service of psychic qualities, creators of domination, who should watch carefully over their own acts, so that their example may be, for the persons over whom they have an influence, a source of improvement and constant elevation."

Lesson VI
By Psychic Influence

Psychic influence consists in awakening the forces, too often wasted by a habitual state of moral weakness, or perhaps lessened from a physiological cause.

It is the power that determines the processes that we wish to produce in other minds.

It is the art of substituting for the want of resolution in others our own will, which they obey blindly, sometimes unconsciously, ever glad to feel themselves guided and directed by a moral power which they can not elicit in themselves.

"It is not necessary," says Yoritomo, "to have, as many pretend, recourse to magic in order to become past masters in the art of influencing others; what is needed above all is to keep ourselves constantly in a condition of will-power sufficient to impose our commands on minds capable only of obedience.

"Intensity of determination, when it reaches a certain point, possesses a dazzling influence which few ordinary mortals can resist, for it envelops them before they are aware of it and thus before they have dreamt of endeavoring to withdraw themselves from it.

"Moreover, those who retain the power of influencing rarely need to exert themselves, in order to exercise it effectually, for the need of protection from it is non-existent in most persons.

"They are rare who are morally sufficient for themselves and who pass through life without feeling the need of resting their weakness on a supporting and directing force.

"Still less numerous are those who accept with courage the consequences of their acts and do not seek to place the responsibility for these acts on an outside influence, which, however, they are ready to repudiate if they are successful.

"But, should failure come, they will hasten to ascribe the causes to their advisers, proclaiming loudly that, if they had not been impelled to give ear to them, the disaster would not have come about.

"Timidity, while not influenced by the same motives, often leads those who suffer from it to such a dread of responsibility that they arrive at the point of being unable to act, except under the shelter of an impelling power, the manifestation of which seems to them indispensable for excusing their activities.

"We might well pass over in silence persons of bad faith, although they constitute an important group among those who seek the cooperation of others.

"But this sickly dependence on others is with them only adopted by design.

"Feeling themselves incapable of achieving anything by their own efforts, they are content to enjoy the fruit of the exertions of others, for they can always take credit to themselves for the best part, by throwing into the shade those who have a far better right to commendation than themselves.

"I once knew two brothers who were devoted to the study and explanation of the ancient inscriptions graven in temples by the hand of primitive faith.

"The younger of these brothers was verbose, very superficial, but a very brilliant and learned talker.

"The other, continually engrossed, kept himself almost entirely out of sight, uttered only words absolutely necessary, and, when questioned on his science, replied so simply that people pitied his brother for being burdened with such an obvious nonentity.

"The latter, however, won the, good graces of every one by never speaking of his elder brother except with respect and by displaying a certain uneasiness when his learning was discussed.

"In spite of everything, he was obliged to admit he alone was learned, and his brother too shallow to take any other role than that of copyist; but it was perceived that this declaration hurt his brotherly feelings, and the esteem conceived for him increased the more.

"Now the day came when the elder brother vanished into the spirit world; his death passed almost as unnoticed as his life, and no one dreamed of regretting him, when a serious mistake was discovered in a much-disputed text. Of course, the error fell on the memory of the copyist, that useless person whom the kindness of his brother had wished to class among the learned.

"The survivor appeared so affected by this that he gave up his work for some time, and his utterances grew dull and commonplace.

"Nevertheless, at the instance of his friends, he undertook the translation of some ancient Buddhist prayers of immense religious and archeological interest.

"Great was the general astonishment. The grossest errors were combined in this work with the most palpable ignorance; in short, it was impossible to doubt of this: not only had the dead brother alone merit, but he had also the gifts of influencing the younger, for, under the dazzling action of the elder one's thought, the other had been able to reflect himself to the extent of imposing on every one."

And Yoritomo adds:

"It is unquestionable that, by throwing off the effluvia of a sound mental perception, we are able to obtain results which material efforts would achieve with more difficulty.

"Nevertheless, it is sometimes indispensable to avail ourselves of other powerful means in order to put in vibration the forces which surround us and must cooperate in the creation of the result which we wish to attain.

"Every one knows that certain orders uttered during a sleep which we have brought on continue after waking in the form of an obsession, at first confused, afterward dim, but gaining in definiteness and at length tenacious, and, I should say, almost instinctive.

"The quickest and most scientific method of obtaining this sleep is the condition of torpor produced by a look, in which we have learned to embody the fascination of our influence.

"I have already mentioned the power of this look, but we shall increase it in a remarkable degree, if we can succeed in approaching the persons whom we wish 'to influence by lightly touching their shoulders with our hands, turning the thumbs toward their necks and the finger-tips on their vertebral columns.

"If we are afraid to display too much the desire of influencing, and wish to avoid provoking a shrinking back, whether voluntary or not, it will be well to proceed by standing behind the persons whom we wish to put to sleep and, chatting the while, place both hands on their shoulders.

"But this procedure is more difficult to put in practice, for the application of the hands must last more than a minute in order to be efficacious.

"In any case, the experiment can only succeed if it is accompanied by the putting forth of a strong and fixed power of will.

"If you give to your thought the strength and fixity required, even though the persons whom you wish to put to sleep should not succumb to slumber, they would none the less become utterly subject to the mental processes which you have willed to arouse in them.

"But a single second of distraction would render all your exertions vain.

"In order to obviate this failure, it is then well to give to the thought a tangible shape and not to abandon it to a meditative condition; it must take on the features of the object of the desire which you wish to inspire.

"For example, you desire to inculcate in some one the love of science, make a picture in your mind, representing him or her bending over manuscripts, or in the dim light of crypts, see that person engaged attentively in deciphering inscriptions, and seeking their meaning, that veritable key of the door from which the truths of history emerge.

"If you wish to imbue them with the warlike spirit, imagine them confronting enemies whom they are crushing to earth.

"Similarly with every accomplishment the idea of which you wish to see born in their minds.

"At the same time, it is absolutely necessary to accentuate and to sustain the thought by words that rouse and stimulate it, by a definite enunciation of it.

"For example, you will say to the person whom you wish to render brave and resolute:

"'Lift your head and accustom yourself to look danger in the face; flee not, it would pursue you and surely overtake you; but know how to measure yourself with it and confront it with a countenance unblanched with fear. . . .'

"It is with such words uttered in a firm voice, the while using the influence of the eye, that of the thought and that of the will, combined with the power of the fluids, that you will succeed in subjugating the most rebellious natures and in making the most inattentive give ear.

"Leaders should never lose sight of this truth: the effort of the will produces vibratory waves the circulation of which must touch the brain of those whom they wish to subjugate.

"To allow this force the means of unbending a little, it is well, when you engage in conversation, to remain quiet while the others talk.

"While listening to them with attention you will avoid looking at the speakers and, without affectation, turn your eyes from theirs in order not to allow to be scattered the fluid which later you will send forth more efficaciously, if, instead of submitting involuntarily to the sway of the speech coming from your interlocutor, you reserve the accumulation of your psychic forces to support your discourse with all the power of occult insight.

"This must be strictly observed when it involves imposing a definite resolution, such as to deter one from a blamable action, or one contrary to that which you desire to see follow.

"Then persuasion by influence takes the form of suggestion, and, after having had recourse to the practices which we have just described, you should say, fixing your eyes, not on but between the bridge of the nose: 'You will not do such or such a thing, because that is bad and would draw you into grievous ills'; or: 'You must do such a thing, there is the solution of the problem which you seek.'

"If the desired result should not be obtained after a first trial, you should renew it. It is, however, preferable to press home the conviction gradually; it thereby gains solidity, and the vacillation, so common in feeble minds, is less to be feared in proportion as the suggestion has been slow in affirmation."

The Shogun deals also with the health of the body, which, he assures us, is always related to that of the mind, and recommends means for assisting the cure of certain sick persons.

Nevertheless, he advises the greatest care in the use of these agencies, however beneficent they may be.

"It is bad," he says, "roughly to compel imaginary invalids to recognize moral error, the prime cause of physical ailments.

"We should, on the contrary, refrain—from denying the existence of their sufferings and, little by little, introduce into their minds the suggestion of something better, until the moment when the idea of recovery gains possession of them.

"But in order to acquire a definite value, this idea must be the culmination of a series of other thoughts the upward gradation of which has led the patients to conceive, at first as a possibility, then as a well-grounded hope, afterward as a certainty, at last as a realization, the complete return of health definitely regained."

"Influence is synonymous with 'substitution of will'; in certain cases, the word 'creation' would be still more appropriate, for those whom we have succeeded in dominating to the extent of directing their thoughts are nearly always persons of weak character in whom the faculty of volition has remained in a rudimentary state.

"As for the others, those in whose minds we substitute our own will for that which they tend to manifest, they are generally dull or frankly vicious souls, who combine with their natural defects a kind of moral weakness, which renders them accessible to outside influence.

"When two forces come together, it is oftener the evil one that gives way, for, to possess the genuine endowment of influence, certain qualities must come into play which rarely fall to the lot of mediocre minds.

"The latter, fatally enslaved to the satisfaction of their instincts, and their strength sapped with fleeting pleasures, lack that impassioned desire of the better, the creator of the cohesion of forces.

"The masters of conscious will alone can hope to arrive at this splendid goal of influencing others, for, their spirit being imbued with nothing but the love of truth, they will ignore those passing whims that ever imprint falsehood or deceit on the thought of those who love to stray along the devious bypaths of unworthy considerations.

"The latter must never hope to possess completely the power of dominance, for they ignore the unity of thought, inasmuch as their mouth utters one word while their mind conceives another; thus the image can not take shape in them except in an imperfect fashion, and we know how important a part that plays which we might call, in a way, the materialization of the idea in the art of influencing others."

"It is not given to all to possess in themselves the aggressive spirit necessary to command the influences which must emanate from our brain in order to result in forming the convictions of others; that is why it is sometimes well, instead of commanding the idea, to let it simply penetrate by itself, in order that we may arrive at its complete possession, which should not be confounded with the fact of being possessed by it.

"The difference is immense: those who possess completely the idea which they wish afterward to send out by the means which we have described in this chapter, in order to transmit the idea to others, are true leaders. Those who allows themselves to be overcome by the obsession of an idea which takes possession of their brains and prevents their reasoning is the slave of that idea and of the acts which it will impel them to commit.

"But this cannot be, if quietly and by degrees, they allow themselves to be imbued with it, for the gradual conquest implies discussion, reasoning, and even resistance, things all indispensable to the formation of rational conviction.

"Now, without conviction, influence has little weight.

"It is personal conviction which allows us to find the words necessary to introduce it into the minds of our hearers; only personal conviction can produce adepts.

"All apostles have been persuaded of the truth of their belief, and, if some among them have been the leaders of the multitude, it is because they taught a doctrine in which they themselves sincerely believed and because their discourse spread around them the radiance of fervor, which, far better than enthusiasm, can fill people's souls and influence them.

"The gradual penetration of the idea is, therefore, to be sought in the case of those whom their natural qualities incline rather to meditation and steady adherence than to aggressive zeal.

"We might compare these different characters to those two men who, having each obtained an equal supply of wood in the forest, returned home and lit the fire to warm themselves.

"One of them let the flames mount in beautiful spiral curves of prismatic color, and when they died down he threw in a fresh armful, delighted with the pleasure of the sight and with the bodily comfort of the warmth.

"But soon nothing remained with which to renew the fire; the flames died away; the ruddy fire took on a vesture of gray, then a fine ash, rapidly cooling, alone remained at the bottom of the fireplace.

"The man went out again to find a fresh supply; but in passing before the hut of his friend he was astonished to see smoke arising from it, while, near the threshold, the pile of wood still lay, but little diminished.

"He went in; an agreeable warmth took possession of him and he saw a modest fire gently smoldering under the ashes; all around people were standing stretching their hands for the genial sensation that pleasantly imbued them.

"So it is with gradual and continuous penetration; if it does not produce brilliant flashes, it bathes us with its beneficent suggestion, and persuaded at last that we bear within us the truth, it will be so much the easier for us to surround ourselves with all the means that the knowledge of influence places at our disposal for allowing this truth to filter gently into the minds of those who would seem to us worthy of understanding it and of spreading it in their turn."

Lesson VII
By Decision

We should not confuse the virtue of decision with that tendency which certain persons display to decide any question whatsoever without having studied it and too often without having understood it.

Like all qualities, decision is only acquired after repeated acts of reflection, determining the coordination of ideas and rendering those who devote themselves to it habitually ready to understand in a moment the advantages, at the same time as they perceive the disadvantages, of the acts which they purpose to perform.

To attain this, we must take into account all the reasons indispensable for evolving decision,

"These reasons," said Yoritomo, "are always dependent on circumstances which constantly assume a new character; for it is rarely indeed that in our lives the necessity for the selfsame resolution makes itself felt on several occasions; even in the case in which the present emergency seems to reproduce exactly a former event, we shall find in the manner of viewing it, in the forecasting of the consequences, even in the gradual change of our feelings, a number of fine distinctions, which do not allow us to form the same opinion about it that we have in the past.

"In order to be able to discern and understand quickly to which side our decision ought to incline, in order above all to be able to sustain it, several qualities are necessary, at the head of which we should name:

"Reflection or concentration.

"Presence of mind.

"Will.

"Energy.

"Impartiality.

"Desire of justice.

"Forethought.

"*Reflection*, or rather *concentration*, is the faculty of self-recollection, of shutting ourselves away from every thought that is not the one that should engage our attention.

"It is force that we bear within ourselves, but which we develop to its highest degree by cultivation and application.

"It is by the habit of reflection by which we succeed in reviewing very rapidly every side of a question and in weighing the pros and cons of the resolutions to be taken.

"This habit, when it is constant, becomes a kind of mental gymnastics and allows us to range together in the twinkling of an eye the reasons which militate in favor of the conclusion, or those which should decide the abandonment of the project which is proposed to us.

"When the balance carries it strongly to one side or the other, the decision is plainly indicated, but many cases arise in which the reasons in favor are quite as important and as numerous as those against, so that the undecided person stops to weigh them interminably.

"Those of us whom the regular practice of *reflection* has perfected, after having rapidly established this equilibrium, will withdraw our minds from these motives in order to summon others of a different order.

We will bring in questions of family, of convenience, of surroundings, we will weigh the consequences of acceptance against the inconvenience of refusal, and we will make up our minds in a clear fashion and one devoid of any regret.

"Now comes in the second factor—*Will*.

"It is sometimes very hard to reply by refusal to something which, in the midst of dangerous advantages, presents seductive aspects; it is painful also to undertake certain responsibilities and to bind oneself to onerous conditions.

"But those of us who are gifted with *will* accept this task with a light heart, for we know that we are worthy of discharging it

"However, this faculty, that admirable origin of the forces that govern life, does not always suffice to fortify decisions, it needs, in order to sustain them, to call to its aid *energy*, which, by continuousness of effort, comes to prevent they faintness which might affect these decisions as time goes on.

"Is there need to insist on *impartiality*, the exercise of which is indispensable when considering one's innermost self?

"The majority of the irresolute love to deceive themselves by the delusions which their imagination creates, and thus become only too often the architects of their own misfortune.

"Or again the decision, sometimes too sudden, is dictated to them by one reason alone, which, with their tacit participation, takes on such gigantic proportions that it hides all the disadvantages, which they embellish, if they are forced to perceive them, with colors which they know to be fictitious.

"*Sincerity* is also necessary with ourselves as with others, and those who do not practice it regret sooner or later having disregarded it.

"It is from the same principle that the *desire of justice* proceeds, which should predominate in all our decisions, if we wish that they bring us no remorse.

"Blundering selfishness can only dictate resolutions which have no foundation in rectitude, for, sooner or later, regrets will arise for the acts that inevitably follow, and the concatenation of events will become the punishment of those who have neglected the laws of the love of their neighbor.

"The principal condition of decisions that leave no bitterness behind is the *foreseeing* of the events which these decisions may elicit.

"To foresee is to prevent, says an ancient maxim, and for want of foresight we often entrust ourselves to a quicksand where, in spite of every effort, we are miserably engulfed.

"We should not confound forethought with the art of divination, although, in the eyes of the vulgar, it sometimes takes on the appearance of it.

"Such persons, adepts in rational reflection, are so advanced in this science that deduction takes the place of second sight, and they succeed in formulating predictions which might pass for prophecies, if they did not themselves take care to explain in what manner they have come to form their judgment.

"It is related that an ancient Mikado, pursued by ill fortune, assembled his soothsayers in order to obtain from them the means of averting the anger of the malignant spirits.

"After much discussion, they agreed that the only means of attaining this was to build a temple consecrated to the gods of Evil, in order to appease them by paying them honor; this temple was to be built on a spot indicated by the magicians.

"However, a preliminary sacrifice was demanded by the merciless gods; a child was to be slain and the temple to be erected on the place crimsoned by its blood.

"After lengthy cabalistic incantations, it was decided that this child should be the first whom chance led them to meet at daybreak in the neighboring forest.

"So the Mikado set out with the sorcerers and a numerous retinue.

"The sun had just risen over the horizon, when they saw through the branches a child walking and making a way for himself through the denseness of the thicket.

"To seize him and lead him to the Mikado was the work of a moment; the poor child was immediately subjected to an examination by the magicians who all agreed in declaring that his blood would be agreeable to the evil gods, and he was committed to the soldiers, who dragged him after them, cruelly divulging to him what would be the tragic end of his captivity.

"Neither prayers nor supplications availed to move any of these fanatics, and the party pursued its course as far as the foot of a hill that overlooked the sea.

"Arrived at this point, the Mikado and his retinue stopped, for it had been decided to choose the flat land covering this hill for the building of the temple.

"The soldiers began to convey thither an enormous stone which, after serving as an altar of human sacrifice was to be the foundation of the edifice.

"The child, seized with an anguish quite comprehensibly, followed with attention all these preparations; but in proportion as he formed an explanation of the work of the soldiers, his countenance cleared, an expression of hope lit up his face, and in a little while he asked permission to speak. Permission being granted him, he bowed three times before the Mikado and cried:

"'O great prince, do not allow the work undertaken to proceed, for the gods of the forest are opposed to it.'

"The Mikado who was superstitious, but not wicked, looked at him sadly.

"'Child,' said, he, 'our soothsayers have decided it thus; it is the only means of appeasing the anger of the malignant spirits whose evil influences threaten the safety of the throne; it is painful to me to sacrifice so young a life, but the welfare of my empire depends on it; resign thyself and die bravely, in order to enter the realm reserved for the valorous.'

"During this address, the child followed attentively the movements of the soldiers and all at once uttered a cry:

"'Command them to stop, great prince, for a few steps farther and the gods of the forest will destroy them.'

"And turning toward the densely wooded forest:

"'Gods of my childhood,' he entreated, 'ye who have ever protected me, give me a fresh proof of your beneficent protection by engulfing up my tormentors together with the altar on which they would sacrifice me.'

"Hardly had he uttered these words than, as if by magic, the soldiers who were pushing forward the heavy stone disappeared—stone and all had been drawn into the bowels of the earth by an invisible power. The assemblage cried out at the miracle and hastened to cut the bonds of the captive, who was lost forthwith in the depths of the forest.

"It had sufficed him, for saving his life, to remember that, when pasturing his goats, he had been stopped by quicksand, which, had it not been for his nimbleness and lightness, would have made him their prey.

"To foresee that men rolling a heavy block of stone could not avoid being swallowed up, was thus easy for him, and this child accustomed to the devices of the simple, which at every moment must protect their lives, had contracted, in the solitudes of the forests, the habit of rapid decision in all that concerns this instinct of self-preservation, so highly developed in all primitive minds.

"Threatened with immolation by those who wished to appease barbarous gods, his astuteness had forced on him the quick decision to strike awe into their minds by prophesying an event which foresight caused him to view as inevitable.

"This is the case of many soothsayers, but it is above all that of sages, who only undertake an enterprise after they have foreseen its difficulties.

"Cells formed spontaneously as the result of chance are too often produced by circumstances.

"If it is difficult to foresee their nature, it is absolutely necessary to recognize them under the vague name of bad luck and to take into account their happening, in order not to be taken by surprise when they burst upon us."

In turning over a few more pages, we come upon a definition of decision, couched in brief and concise phraseology, such as the Nippon philosophy knows how to employ when it would sum up a thought in such a manner as to impress the mind.

"Decision," he said, "is not a spontaneous movement of the mind or of the intelligence, it is the coherent and rational choice of performing an act to the exclusion of all others which might bear a relation to the idea expressed."

And he adds:

"Between the moment when the reason for the decision appears and that in which it is a question of making the resolve, all the psychic states which separate these two periods find place.

"We have just enumerated them rapidly, but in order to grasp them in their integrity and to make them serve for the accomplishment of our projects maturely conceived and rapidly inaugurated, a kind of mental gymnastics is not unprofitable.

"For example, it is well to place ourselves in face of imaginary resolutions and to make up our minds while striving to do so as speedily and wisely as possible.

"It will be easy for us to measure the wisdom of our resolutions, if we take as our end the events which surround us and if we study the delicate cases which are within reach of our knowledge.

"It is well, on seeing arise among our friends circumstances of which we have no experience, to make use of them as a subject for our exercises and to say to ourselves: 'What decision should I make if I were faced with this problem?'

"I do not say, mind you, that all the details of the facts would become known to you in such a way that it would be possible to reason from them with certainty.

"This method has the advantage of a check, for it allows you to verify the success of the decisions which you have made in imaginary cases.

"You can thus instruct yourself in this art, so difficult and nevertheless so important, for the influence which those who are accustomed to wise and prompt decisions exert over others is always considerable.

"Further, when some time you devote yourself to this study, you will come to make it naturally and without any effort.

"Clearness of mental vision will develop within you to such a point that, without giving it a thought, you will come to pass a sound judgment on everything and to discern quickly what is the solution proper to each.

"Soon the fame of your wisdom will spread abroad and the weak-willed ones will come to gather around you to ask your counsel.

"For they are numerous who dare not venture alone in the paths of will—the creator of responsibilities.

"Their craven souls fear the regrets arising from a resolution of which they would have to bear the consequences." He then related this allegorical adventure:

"'A man,' he said, 'had to pass through a forest in order to reach a village where he hoped to meet Fortune.

"'He set out very early in the morning and hastened to reach as quickly as possible the outskirts of the forest.

"'But when he had walked for some hours, he stopped and looked around him in indecision; the road laid out was long and monotonous; by taking a by-path across the wood he had perhaps a chance to shorten it . . . and he lost his way under the great trees.

"'He walked on for an hour and found himself in a glade. He tried to get his bearings, but, not knowing what to do, he took a road by chance. He went more slowly, for he began to feel fatigue and became quite dejected, when he perceived that the road had brought him back quite near to the point whence he had set out.

"'He then took the opposite road, but he could not keep count of the windings that it made, so that after a long course he saw the glade again.

"'That was for him the moment of a great resolution, he gave up definitely the side roads and set out on the first road which he had followed and which led directly to the village.

"'But the sun set behind the trees; night covered the forest with its veil, and the distracted man was obliged to interrupt his journey, now useless, for Fortune had failed to wait for him.'

"Do not laugh at this man," cried the Shogun, "you are for the most part like him; you wander in the labyrinths of indecision instead of following the way pointed cut by the will; you lose your presence of mind at the first objection; you avoid being sincere with yourselves by avowing that you heedlessly lose your way in unknown roads, and when at length you pause before a definite course, opportunity has wearied of waiting for you.

"Despise these irresolute ones, ye who aspire to become those whose influence radiates over the souls of others.

"Be counselors with well-weighed and prompt decisions; do not stray in the by-paths of which you do not know the windings, and learn to become safe and enlightened guides for yourselves before pointing out the way to those of whom your influence has made attentive and devoted disciples."

It seems that to add any comment to these teachings would be to risk weakening them, for these appeals burning with energy, as well as the luminous illustrations that accompany them, can serve as a rule of conduct for the people of this day as well as for the far-distant disciples of Yoritomo.

Lesson VIII

By Rational Ambition

Ambition is accessible only to the brave; they alone can discover the treasure hidden within it, by breaking up the sham gems of illusion and intrigue.

These words of Yoritomo should be known to all those who set out for the conquest of life.

They should be inscribed in letters of gold on the frontals of schools where the young make the initial start that, in most cases, decides their future.

"Ambition," again says the old philosopher, "should, equally with goodness or any other virtue, form the object of rational teaching.

"But for that it would be necessary to disengage ourselves from prejudices which brand it as a fault which we ought to dissemble.

"'He or she is an ambitious one,' say the vulgar, when they wish to discredit the achievements of a person whose aspirations raise that person above the commonplace things of life.

"They do not dream that, in order to form a genuine and productive ambitious person, it is necessary to possess a great number of qualities which people who pride themselves on their modesty, will always ignore.

"What is understood generally by modesty?

"Is it the shrewd reserve of ambitious people who fear to display their appetites in order not to be liable to restrain them before having found the means of satisfying them?

"Is it not too often the sham virtue which, under the borrowed lineaments of humility, hides the terrible defect of weakness?

"Would it not rather be the tinsel in which idleness likes to dress itself up in order to abandon itself with ease to its favorite vice?

"Modesty can serve as a standard for all the vices which we have just mentioned; it is the enemy of courageous undertakings, of acts that require a display of energy that ambition or boldness alone can decide on.

"It is besides nearly always the sign of a want of confidence in oneself.

"It is again the safeguard of the self-respect of the incapable.

"Many weak mortals, irresolute, idle, or incompetent, instead of seeking to acquire the qualities which they lack, prefer to declare loudly: 'Oh, as for me, I shall never succeed in attaining this end, for the good reason that I shall not undertake it. I am a modest person, *I* am. I have a hatred of fame and renown surrounding my name; I desire only obscurity, and I pity keenly all those who are tormented by a desire to shine!

"They say all this without thinking that the first condition of the being of modesty consists in ignorance of its existence.

"Those who pride themselves on modesty will never be truly modest, for the moment they set out to establish their virtue they act like braggarts.

"If they are really convinced of their unimportance, if their diffidence is sincere, we should pity them very keenly, for they will suffer in feeling so insignificant, and this feeling will lead, little by little, to hypochondria, unless they incline to the side of jealousy.

"Such is almost without exception the punishment of the weak; they have not themselves courage to undertake great things and they do not forgive those who achieve them.

"There is, however, a kind of modesty before which we ought to bow; it is that of the learned person who, finding happiness in the quest of knowledge and truth, makes no attempt to gain glory, and waits in the midst of his or her apparatus and parchments for it to develop, while preparing to welcome it with no more emotion than an ordinary visitant.

"This sentiment would be worthy of admiration if it were not so often mingled with an inveterate selfishness, behind which is hidden an indifference toward others, carried to the point of excluding anxiety to cause others to share in the benefit of one's discoveries.

"This kind of modest person who ignores thus his or her duty toward others is less useful to humanity than an ambitious person, who, eager to become famous, will make known the result of what is accomplished to the sound of the trumpet.

"For in order to be fruitful, everything in our life must bear relation to others.

"It is by developing ambition in their breasts that the leaders of the multitude have succeeded first in gaining a hearing and then in carrying conviction.

"What generous impulse can we expect from those who have only one desire; to shut themselves up in the selfish quiet of a life the works of which they jealously keep to themselves?"

These facts, already true enough in the days of the Shogun, assume a fresh significance in our time, when they might become the textbook of those whom we designate by the name of those who have arrived and who are in the majority of cases nothing if not ambitious ones—I was almost going to say the rightfully ambitious.

And why? Ambition, when it excludes unworthy means and spurns intrigue, is it not one of the noblest passions that could be conceived?

National ambition furnishes our projects with wings that allow them to mount above commonplace ideas; it is thanks to ambition that we experience emulation that carries us along the better way.

Without ambition should we have knowledge of those marvelous discoveries that make our age that of progress *par excellence*? And it might be said that Yoritomo set forth the splendid incentives given to the ambitious of our time by benefactors keen beyond measure on improvement, when he says:

"It is a crime to destroy in the breasts of children, under the pretense of modesty, that self-confidence which should shine like a star in the hearts of all.

"It would be more useful, on the contrary, to found rewards for distribution to those who, with a noble end in view, devote themselves to undertakings sometimes called rash.

"Such are the veritable handmaids of destiny, since, by their desire for the better, they sometimes succeed in discovering an improvement which ameliorates the lot in life of others . . .

"Besides, it is well that every effort should be rewarded by an increase in the possessions of those who have made the attempt and who, by their special qualifications, have promoted a success the good results of which are never limited to themselves.

"Justice demands that inventors should derive profit from their inventions, this will allow them to devote more of their time to the pursuit of another discovery."

It will perhaps be objected that there are some ambitious people who produce nothing. Those whose success profits only themselves and who cannot spread around them the joy which arises from generous benefactions.

The world is certainly peopled with a large number of selfish persons and it will assuredly be difficult to prevent this state of things, but it would be a serious mistake to believe that these people are altogether useless.

Ambition is never without the great desire of attaining everything which gratifies it, and what better means is there of proclaiming its success than to command a large retinue, to give banquets, and to build palaces, or plant spacious gardens?

Even granting that ambitious people who have attained satisfaction are hard-hearted and neglect works of charity, do not the workers who labor in providing the trappings of their vanity profit largely by an ambition which procures for them the means of subsistence?

By the law of human evolution, the money obtained by the ambitious will come of necessity to ameliorate the condition of the humble, in the same way as their works and their discoveries will always succeed in increasing the fund of public knowledge, for only modest people are able to keep to themselves the result of their labors.

Those who would master fame or fortune, on the other hand, hastens to make public the most trifling success; true, they sometimes exaggerate it, but the fault is not theirs alone; it may be imputed to the habit of disparaging those on whom Fortune seems to smile.

"I heard one day," said the Shogun, "a man whom I knew to be of a serious turn of mind relate that he had spent three years in completing a work.

"Now I had followed his studies with interest, and I knew that this task had required of him in all a hundred and fifty days.

"I was, therefore, astonished, and questioned him on the reason of a falsehood which puzzled me the more that I knew his habitual truthfulness.

"'Child,' replied he, 'do you not understand that if I were to admit spending so little time in perfecting my work people would not fail to find it incomplete or too lightly thought out? It is not sufficient to be capable, we must not shock any one in proving overmuch this capability. For this assertion of a quality that they do not possess causes suffering in the envious who do not fail to revenge themselves for it by belittling it to others. It is their method of succeeding in placing themselves in the same class; unable to rise to the level of people of merit, they try to bring the latter down to their level.'"

Ambitious people escape these cheap devices; they are from the first too full of their projects to give time to insignificant jealousies.

In short, they rarely resent the sentiment of envy, for they are always convinced that they will succeed in surpassing the success of those who are competing for the same goal.

Moreover, ambition is a sure and swift means of influence.

This is, in the first place, because people have always a tendency to follow those who draw them in the direction of light and progress.

Those are chosen to attain honors and fortune are almost always drawn from the following of the ambitious.

It forms no part of the program of the successful ones to drag after them the incapable or weak; this is why their influence over their pupils extends the more in proportion as the latter imitate and follow them.

For ambitious people are not displeased to see disciples raise themselves and perhaps some day step into their vacant place. And here is one of the primary reasons for the influence which rational ambition can exert on the minds of people.

The lure of gain or distinction binds people to the train of those who are in a position to give such away to them.

It is in their power to be able to employ this influence profitably for disseminating good and the love of the better around them; it is in their power to instill into the hearts of their devotees aspirations toward a noble end; it is in their power always to put them on their guard against intrigues which would have the effect of diminishing the beauty of their ambition.

There is between ambitious people and intriguers all the difference that separates beauty from ugliness.

The first proceed, directly toward a definite goal that they have long and maturely decided to choose; they disdain paltry methods; they seek only to attain the end that they have set up.

They move ahead with full confidence, sustained by a faith that is never lost from view, notwithstanding the clouds that hide it from time to time.

They ignore the vulgar herd of the envious who swarm around them, unless, overmuch beset or tormented by their incessant attacks they crush them under foot, as we do with an importunate insect, which we try at first to drive away and which we destroy, without ill feeling, simply to rid ourselves of its repeated and irritating stings.

Intriguers, on the other hand, rarely raise themselves above the horde of mean desires and paltry jealousies.

Unlike their ambitious counterparts, they act with no other end in view than the procuring for themselves money or pleasure.

No lofty thought ever enter their heads longer than the time necessary to turn it to account, while considering only its mercenary aspect, and this accomplished, they pass to a class of ideas the burden of which is ever the same.

The desire of distinction never haunts the dreams of intriguers; they reduce everything to the narrowness of their aspirations and entertains no project that does not lend itself to their base sentiments.

Is that to say that we should despise money and seek after poverty?

"Not so," said Yoritomo, "for the poor person exercises little influence over the multitude.

"Again, most achievements demand considerable application and loss of time, and we could not lavish it in this way if we were obliged to take thought for the earning of our daily bread.

"It is, therefore, well to find resources that will allow the pursuit of an end without being compelled to give it up in order to provide for the necessities of daily life. This will also save us from compromises of conscience which the greatest leaders must sometimes endure, when they do not possess that advantage, indispensable to those who do not wish to diverge from their course—assurance as to the primary needs of life.

"This should be the first aim of those who wish to win honor, fortune, or distinction.

"Before rushing forth on toilsome paths on the chance of meeting such, we should be sure of the possibility of pursuing them and not risk missing them because the necessity of providing for our daily wants compels us to pause just when we had hoped to attain them."

We can not but admire once again the wisdom of Yoritomo, who once more is found in agreement with the greatest thinkers.

The ancient Greek poet, Theognis said: "The man who is broken down by poverty can neither speak nor act; his tongue is tied and his feet are chained."

It is only too true; downright poverty is a disadvantage, for it often compels those who suffer to pay court to the fortunate ones of this world.

In any case, it is a hindrance to all undertakings that require sustained effort and peace of mind, which can only be obtained by those certain of the morrow.

But, you will say, everybody cannot be rich, and many, becoming so, have known poverty; is it not then an insuperable obstacle?

Again the Shogun will reply to us:

"Poverty," said he, "is a hindrance only if it consists in absolute want, and in this case it is usually the result of idleness or of mismanagement of our affairs.

"We should not reckon as poor people who earn a scanty livelihood but whose peace of mind cannot be changed by the suffering resulting from the lack of necessaries.

"Such people can, when they have fulfilled the duties of their station in life, devote themselves to the aspirations of a lawful ambition.

"But the really poor are those who lack assured means, however small.

"Rarely do they enjoy independence, for in order to live they must accept many humiliations or spend a considerable portion of time in quests which have as their object the insurance of sustaining a livelihood.

"If they are sincere in these efforts, they will not long remain poor, for they will soon find employment, no matter what, and if endowed with ambition they will quickly succeed in distinguishing themselves in it.

"From that time, poverty will be nothing but a specter of the past, for they will work to better their positions and will soon become successful."

Prosperity begins in the mind and is impossible while the mental attitude is hostile to it.

It is fatal to work for one thing and to expect something else, because everything must be created mentally first and is bound to follow its mental pattern.

You can never become prosperous if you expect to remain poor. We tend to get what we expect, and to expect nothing is to get nothing. When every step you take is on the road to failure, how can you hope to arrive at the success goal?

It is the facing the wrong way toward the black, depressing, hopeless outlook, even though we may be working in the opposite direction that kills the results of our effort.

Thoughts are magnets that attract things like themselves. If your mind dwells upon poverty and disease, it will bring you poverty and disease. There is no possibility of your producing just the opposite of what you are holding in your mind, because your mental attitude is the pattern, which is built into your life. Your accomplishments are achieved mentally first.

The terror of failure and the fear of coming to want and of possible humiliation keep multitudes of people from obtaining the very things they desire, by sapping their vitality and incapacitating them, through worry and anxiety, for effective, creative work necessary to give them success.

The habit of looking at everything constructively, from the bright, hopeful side, the side of faith and assurance, instead of from the side of doubt and uncertainty; and the habit of believing the best is going to happen, that the right must triumph; the faith that truth is bound finally to conquer error, that harmony and health are the reality and discord and disease the temporary absence of it—this is the attitude of the optimist, which will ultimately reform the world.

I have never known anyone who believed in him or herself and constantly affirmed this ability to do what was undertaken, who always focused on the goal and struggled determinedly toward it, who did not make a success of life. *Aspiration becomes inspiration and then realization.*

"Poverty is only allowable if it is voluntary, that is to say, if it is the result of a decision which prefers that condition to another more brilliant but less independent.

"Nevertheless, riches are the key of many marvels and they are above all the key of many influences.

"Not only are those of great possessions in a better position to make those whom they patronize listen to their words, but the prestige of their success surrounds them with a halo of influence, which, if they are wise, be will used to better the lot of other people.

"We do not receive kindnesses from an empty hand; we have nothing to expect from a person tormented by care for the morrow.

"What words can fall from a mouth sealed by hunger?"

It is true that fortune, considered simply from the point of view of riches, is not an exalted ideal, but we must nevertheless welcome it as the consecration of success and as a power of which, the sage knows how to dispose for the good of all people.

It is a means of exciting interest and of influencing the multitude, for the people will always be disposed to listen to the advice of those who have had the ability to acquire great possessions.

It is then in the power of those who have been able to acquire this power of money to make use of it for establishing a beneficent influence over the minds of those who are disposed to trust in them.

After their other successes, this last will not be a matter of indifference to those who, while monopolizing the empire of the purse, will be proud to endeavor after the authority of the empire of the mind.

Thanks to the prestige which their riches confer on them, they will be able to spread the rays of influence as far as the boundaries of the attraction of thought, and as it displays itself above all in action they will gather around them a band of brave and intelligent people, ready to imitate them in spreading abroad the ideas which they inculcated in them and to speak as they have taught them.

"Do not wait for the desired object to come to you, but rise up and set out to look for it; when you have found it you will undertake its conquest, and when it becomes your possession you will gather together your friends to make them share in your good fortune and to tell them by what means it has befallen you."

In acting thus, you will follow the teaching of Yoritomo who said:

"Ambition is a gate opening on magnificent gardens, but the fortunate ones who have entered it should not pause there; they will pass beyond the entrance in order to survey the road and to make a sign to passers-by, pointing out to them the way."

And this profound psychologist adds:

"A discovery brings no real joy to its finder until he or she can announce it, and we should rejoice at this almost universal law, for it is the cause of an improvement evolved by ambition, the happy influence of which awakens the instinct of conquest dormant in the breast of every righteous person."

Lesson IX

By Perseverance

Like persuasion, like good example, perseverance is among, if not the most brilliant, at least the most active agents of influence.

It is a faculty borne within them by people conscious of their power, those who, by virtue of faith in their own merit, advance to achievement with that confidence which gives birth to all notable successes and all productive achievements.

Perseverance is the triumph of will-power over the weakness of the will; it is the result of a profound study of the determining causes, the combination of which is bound to end in success; it is, in short, the slow but sure ascent toward a goal that assumes a more definite shape the nearer we approach it.

Few persons are born with a silver spoon in their mouths, but everybody can aim at conquering fortune by a series of continual and rational efforts.

The athlete who would spring up thirty feet at a single leap would spend a lifetime in ridiculous attempts, but if that athlete wishes steadily to mount the steps that lead to that height, it will be attained, sooner or later, according to the dexterity, the agility, and the perseverance which that person displays.

The steps, it is true, are often made of shaky stone; they have gaps between them that make one dizzy, where they are so uncertain that it is difficult to keep a foothold on them.

This is the point where those who possess the virtue of perseverance make themselves known; by their unshakable will they can ward off every danger; they balance themselves on the shaky stones almost on tiptoe and advance onto the next step; they feel fascinated by the giddy depths beneath them, quickly they raise their heads, they proceed gazing on their star, and they guard themselves against possible slips by making sure of one foot before lifting the other from the ground.

Even those with small ability will often succeed if they have the dogged persistence, where a genius without it would fail. Persistence wedded to character is the key to success in life. Money, influence, position are as nothing compared with brains, principle, energy and perseverance.

No one can pursue a worthy object steadily and persistently with all the powers of one's mind, and yet be a failure. Focus the rays of the sun in winter, and you can kindle a fire with ease.

"For perseverance is the mother of many gifts; from her is born circumspection which clasps hands with application and patience.

"It is incredible to what degree the person who is gifted with patience is proof against the pitfalls of fate; hope and cheerfulness are two unanswerable arguments under most circumstances; application comes to hold up their hands, and few undertakings can resist their combined influence.

"It is related that the great scholar Yuan-Shi, plagued by the sour temper of his wife, who was jealous of his knowledge, could find no way of working at home, for this shrew went so far as to throw his manuscripts about and burn the sheets of paper on which he set down his thoughts.

"He therefore resolved, when he was at home to divide his time between gardening and contemplation.

"But from the time that he got into the sedan chair which conveyed him daily from his country house to the town where he was employed, he made up for the time lost by his enforced inactivity; and produced, after some months, a work of great value, which was universally commended and admired.

"News of this reached his wife, who asked him astoundedly how he found the time to write, considering that outside his professorship he was not engaged in any intellectual occupation.

"Yuau-Shi was a simple soul; he related to her how he had managed to reconcile his work with her unreasonableness.

"She was so affected by this proof of his desire not to annoy her, and so impressed by the calm and indomitable will of her husband, that from that day she ceased to forbid him to engage in work which brought him distinction, which shed its rays upon her in the form of caresses that saved her wifely self-respect."

This power persist is characteristic of all people who have accomplished anything great; they may lack in some other particular, have many weaknesses or eccentricities, but the quality of persistence is never absent from successful people. No matter what opposition is faced or what discouragement arises, drudgery cannot disgust them; misfortune, sorrow, and reverses cannot harm them. It is not so much brilliancy of intellect, or fertility of resource, as persistency of effort, constancy of purpose, that make great people.

Those who succeed in life are the men and women who keep everlastingly at it, who do not believe themselves geniuses, but who know that if they every accomplish anything they must do it be determined and persistent industry.

John J. Audubon, the noted American ornithologist tells this story about himself: "An accident which happened to two hundred of my original drawings nearly put a stop to my researches on ornithology. I left the village in which I was living to go to Philadelphia on business. I looked to my drawings before departure, placed them carefully in a wooden box and gave them in charge of a relative with instructions to see that no injury would happen to them. My absence was for several months.

"When I returned I inquired about my box and what I was pleased to call my treasure. The box was produced and opened. To my dismay, a pair of rats had taken possession of the whole and reared a young family among the gnawed bits of paper, which had previously represented drawings of nearly a thousand birds. The burning heat that instantly rushed through my brain was too great to be endured without affecting my entire nervous system. I slept for several nights and the days passed like days of oblivion—until the animal powers being recalled into action through the strength of my constitution, I took up my gun, my notebook and my pencils and went forth into the woods as if nothing had happened. I felt pleased that I might now make better drawings than before. Over the next three years I filled my portfolio again."

This was similar to an experience of Sir Isaac Newton, whose accidental destruction of his papers when his little dog upset a lighted taper upon his desk, by which the elaborate calculations of many years were in a moment destroyed. Although the loss seriously impaired his health and his mind, he persisted in reconstructing the work.

All are familiar with the misfortune of Carlyle while writing his "History of the French Revolution." After the first volume was ready for the press, he loaned the manuscript to a neighbor, who left it lying on the floor, and the servant girl took it to kindle the fire. It was a bitter disappointment, but Carlyle was not one to give up. After many months of poring over hundreds of volumes of authorities and scores of manuscripts, he reproduced that which had burned in a few minutes.

Do we reckon what might be the production of one hour a day won from frivolous pursuits to which we give so many precious minutes, which are so many drops of our life fallen into the gulf of eternity?

"The person," said the Shogun, "who should cut down a branch every day would end by clearing a way through the densest forest."

And he adds judiciously:

"But that person should not think of going back, for the branches grow again and the way would be closed."

That is to say that perseverance must never slacken; return is not allowed to those who should widen the road for their disciples to follow, and we cannot repeat too often.

The giants of the race have been people of concentration, who have struck sledgehammer blows in one place until they have accomplished their purpose. The successful people of to-day are those with one overmastering idea, one unwavering aim, one of single and intense purpose.

Thousands of people have been failures in life because they did not go quite far enough. They fail to walk that extra mile. They did not quite learn a trade to the point of efficiency; in other words, they stopped just this side of success.

It is by the power of personal effort and of application that the most brilliant and, solid reputations are slowly formed.

"Experience," says G. A. Mann, "tells us that we must have, in order to succeed, method in everything that we do and also perseverance; if we do not possess these two qualities we should develop them, and that by thinking constantly of them and by contemplating the idea which represents them.

"Persevere then! To what end, do you say? Simply because by persevering you form your will and besides have the chance of attaining your end.

"Persevere like a brute? Not at all. It is necessary that, in continuing what you have begun, your will, your intelligence, your sensibilities be ever on the alert.

"It is this unceasing activity in yourself that is the reward of your effort.

"The road on which you walk may, perhaps, not lead you where you wished to go. But probably it will lead you to a better place. And for your walk you will become a good walker, which will be certainly due to the impulse that you needed to be able to attain the goal, that is to say, success.

"Will without perseverance and without method could not exist."

Perseverance admits of a combination of active qualities and of virtues that might be called passive, for they demand no apparent effort.

Nevertheless, they are rarer than one might think, for they are not often the endowment of weak minds.

The latter can only with difficulty concentrate themselves on a task that requires a little application; they are the slaves of the instability of their impressions; beginnings, however arduous, always find them full of enthusiasm, but this fervor soon grows cold, and if success does not present itself immediately they will hasten to give up their project and devote themselves to another which will soon have a like ending.

Unremitting action can also be reckoned in the number of these virtues, passive indeed but indispensable, of which we have just spoken.

The practice of bending the will to listen to some purpose is sometimes a talent of a high order, for it is one of the best means of winning the sympathies of those who are speaking with us.

"I hate," said Yoritomo, "the sort of people who let their thoughts wander blindly instead of seeking to glean profit from what they hear.

"Nothing is more disconcerting than to feel the attention of those to whom you are speaking drifting away and wandering after their thoughts, while you would like to convince them by your words.

"This lack of attention is always the mark of a vacillating will which can not bring itself to follow an idea by concentrating its mental powers on an examination of the various aspects which it presents.

"When dealing with inferiors, this frivolous inattention may pass as a sign of contempt; besides, it is always in opposition to the influence which we might exercise over them.

"What should we think of a squire whom a poor peasant comes to consult and who, instead of listening kindly, should pay little attention, as I have often seen, and give orders to servants and arrange the hangings of the house and let musicians go on playing?

"The unfortunate peasant would go out of the squires house with a bad impression, and if ever help or advice was needed in the future, would take care not to go a second time to the squire who treated the request with studied disdain.

"Influence over others is acquired especially by perseverance of the will and concentration of thought, the undulations of which, projected around us, come to reach the minds which we wish to impress."

And, entering once more into the domain of psychology, the Shogun speaks to us of this fascinating mystery of the contagion of thought, which according to him is a primary cause of influence and can not fail by persevering determination to produce it:

"There is no doubt," he said, "that thought is a contagious factor of influence, good or bad.

"Who has not had occasion to remark this in the case of fear?

"In an assemblage composed of the bravest people that it is possible to meet, taken individually, one person stricken with fear, if by expressing this fear in a forcible manner, will succeed in imparting to each of the rest, in different degrees it may be, the disquietude and uneasiness which he or she experiences.

"There are few doughty warriors who at the recital of something concerning the mysteries of the world beyond have not felt a slight shiver which the sight of wholesale carnage, together with the consciousness of the gravest perils, could not have caused them to experience.

"This phenomenon, caused by the irradiation of thought, is an undeniable proof of the influence which it can exercise, for not only is it possible to penetrate the minds touched by the undulations of our own thought, but the thought of others, elicited by ourselves, comes back to us on the same undulations that are spread out from our brain.

"This is why we often see people who wished to shed fear around them feel that same fear by receiving the waves of thought that they have produced in their audience.

"It is the same with laughter.

"Very few are they who can resist the infection of a burst of laughter; even with those least inclined to merriment laughter is infectious in a high degree; for at first involuntary, in a way mechanical, it ends by becoming natural, so that, at the moment it breaks out, the simplest expressions, the most sedate words assume in the imagination so comical an aspect that merriment increases to the point of not being able to utter them without provoking a fresh outburst.

"But what happens if the next day we wish to relate this incident?

"No longer submitted to the attractive influence of the thought of others, no longer receiving from them the undulations, the vibrations of which had reached us on the previous day, our state of mind is completely different, we perceive the inanity (sometimes we should say the foolishness) of what had amused us so highly on the preceding day, and no longer laughing over it ourselves it is impossible for us to entertain others with it.

"On the other hand, if the story-teller—either of set purpose or spontaneously—begins by laughing at the remembrance of what is about to be related, it is seldom that this merriment, if it appears genuine, does not spread to others, who will laugh at first by infection, afterward—of necessity, because merriment is the pervading thought.

"What we have just said on the subject of fear or of laughter applies to everything else.

"With perseverance, you succeed in causing effectively to penetrate the minds of your hearers the thoughts the emission of which will attract similar thoughts, and their undulations returning to affect you will increase your conviction, giving you thus the more power to spread it around you."

It is from this standpoint that the Shogun sets out to oppose the emission of evil thoughts.

"It is" said he, "a weapon which always recoils on those who would make use of it.

"The evil thought traverses the same cycle as the other and returns to us strengthened with hatred for others.

"What can we expect from those in whose minds we cause to germinate wickedness and the desire of evil?

"As soon as they believe themselves capable, it is against us first of all that they will seek to exert themselves, and they will do it involuntarily by bringing back to us our thought, magnified and disfigured, so that we shall endure it without recognizing it.

"You see why perseverance should only be applied to the gaining of good, and as soon as we think we have come into association with it, it will be our duty to inculcate its principles into those who, living around us, are subjected to our influence.

"But we must not limit our efforts to this; we must aim farther and higher; it will not suffice to initiate them into good things, we must also give them the taste to cultivate them, and to that end arouse in them the desire of perseverance, which makes possible the most difficult undertakings and gives us a power that we can not limit.

"Like some steel implement, the drop of water perforates the rock, wears away the hardest stone, and, without slacking, pursues this work which the implement would have begun more successfully perhaps, but the breaking or wearing out of the tool would have interrupted, perforce, the work which the eternal drop of water accomplishes by the tenacity and perseverance of its action.

"Do not then seek to force slow-moving minds, but surround them, penetrate them by your perseverance, and its influence, sometimes obscure but always certain, will spread itself abroad in beneficent undulations, the continuance of which will create power."

Oliver Wendell Holmes expressed this well:

"Never give up, there are chances and changes,
Helping the hopeful, a hundred to one;
And, through the chaos, High Wisdom arranges
Ever success, if you'll only hold on

Never give up; for the wisest is boldest,
Knowing that Providence mingles the cup,
And of all maxims, the best, as the oldest,
Is the stern watchword of 'Never give up!'"

Lesson X

By the Prestige Gained from Concentration

Concentration is one of the most marvelous forces that can be conceived.

Without concentration, no success is possible; if it is present, we must consider it as the work of chance, not reckon too much on its duration, and remember the popular proverb that says:

"The person who comes to the sound of the flute goes back to the sound of the drum."

In other words, what a chance circumstance has brought may depart on the wings of an unforeseen happening.

Far different is the success that we acquire by reason that, having sought it and willed it with all our powers, we have strained every effort to evoke it and no longer hug it to ourselves for fear that it should leave us.

Fidelity to an idea is always the initial step to all successes.

For if an idea has no time to become at home with us, if what is rightly called the crystallization of thought does not form the foundation of every decision, we shall find it impossible to give it definite shape, and it will fade away like impalpable smoke.

If, on the other hand, we know how to exercise concentration, this idea will soon become a focus of organization around which the association of ideas will come to marshal the reasons that determine the action that we have in mind.

"Thoughts are things," said the nineteenth century philosopher, Prentice Mulford. It is easy to imagine how true the saying is, seeing that in thinking deeply on a subject we succeed in picturing it to ourselves in an almost tangible fashion.

The concentrated mind owns itself. It is the divine thinker of its own thoughts, and it declares just what kind of food the mind shall feed upon; it sets a guard upon its field of consciousness and will not allow a thought that is less than constructive to enter in. It picks up the thoughts which will reveal to it a perfect plan of life, then projects a perfect image of that plan and, standing firmly by its own creations, it fashions them again and again with increasing skill, until the whole structure of the self is brought into harmony.

"There is no doubt," said Yoritomo, "that concentration develops all our senses and brings them to a degree of remarkable acuteness.

"It stands to us in the stead of knowledge, for by its means we acquire the facility, that is to say the gift, of realizing readily and easily the things of which we have formed a conception.

"There is no work, even manual, that concentration does not lighten for us.

"If you have to lift a heavy mass, do you think that you will do it as well if you are occupied with some other thought as if you said simply and solely: 'I wish to lift this mass.'

"Then your nerves are at tension, all your faculties bend themselves to the act with a force necessary to perform it; your brain strives after the means to assist the physical effort, for the muscles are the slaves of the will. By concentrating yourself on a manual labor, you are certain to perform it with a minimum of fatigue, for you will be able to husband your strength and will save yourself from dissipating them in useless exertions. You will concentrate all your faculties of attention, of calculation, of ingenuity, and of muscular power in order to succeed.

"This is how so many jugglers achieve perfection in their art; by concentration they have reached such a point of self absorption that for them nothing exists outside their own particular performance.

"But if one day in a fit of passion, they allow their thoughts to wander toward the object of their anger or of their love, they find that they are no longer themselves; their actions become less sure, they make bungle and end by being unable to regain their nerve, except with a violent effort that drives away the fancy and allows them to recall their thoughts to the one point where they should keep them.

"To think of the act which we are performing, to think of it alone, to concentrate everything, and forget everything outside of it, there is the secret of so many successes, the explanation of so many good fortunes, that also of the immense influence which certain people exert over others."

"We must," said the Shogun, "be able to concentrate ourselves on one act at a time and to force our attention to the fullest degree to the manner in which we can attract others to imitate us.

"We are the shapers of our destiny, and we should aspire to become shapers of the destiny of others.

"To gain this end, nothing should appear insignificant to us, and if we think sensibly we shall see that every one of our acts, however commonplace it may seem to us, is, if it is performed with the desire of good, a step toward a realization, sometimes imposing, the fate of which, however, depends on a series of similar acts, equally paltry taken separately, but essential, for the inadequacy of one of them might mar the perfection of the whole, if not jeopardize success altogether."

And in his flowery language the Shogun adds:

"What is one link more or less in a chain several meters long? So trifling a thing that its absence would not be noticed. Nevertheless, if this link is badly riveted, this insignificant detail will suffice to break the chain.

"Every work is made up of a chain of acts more or less infinitesimal; the perfection of each of them contributes to that of the whole and it sometimes suffices for a slight slackness in the performance of one of these acts to jeopardize the success of an undertaking."

In fact, which of us has not had to regret a negligence, which has come to hinder the success of a project?

In our age of electricity and of strenuous life, these remarks are still more true than they would be at any other time.

Does it not happen every day that a missed train causes us the loss of the benefit of some business, which because of the delay escapes us?

Now, if we wish to be perfectly sincere with ourselves, we shall admit that on most occasions this delay is due only to our own carelessness; we were too late for meals, or we wasted time in talk which it would have been quite easy for us to curtail.

All the trouble arose from want of concentration, which allowed us to lose sight of the one thing that should have been for us of the first importance.

If we will reflect well on it, we shall see that most of our troubles can be set down to carelessness.

Take, if you wish, the case that we have just mentioned: A missed train prevents the settlement of an important business.

Thoughtless people will get out of this by saying: "I have not had a chance"; others, those whose thoughts are directed by a master mind, which is an adept at concentration, will recollect themselves, will mentally review all the passing events of the day, and will thereby conclude that they are responsible for that happening so deplorable for their interests.

What then should they do?

Simply devote themselves to one of the exercises most recommended by thinkers; concentrate their faculties on the principal act of the day which was the settlement of the business which called them out, and, once well persuaded of its importance, suit all their acts to it.

They would thus have avoided losing the few minutes or the hour which caused them to fail, for, filled with their determination, they would have cut short any business that it was not indispensable to conclude, or cut off some moments from talk the continuance of which was less important for them than the journey which they had to make.

"Each day," said Yoritomo, "brings with it a round of duties of unequal importance; we must know how to distinguish that which should take precedence, and subordinate to it our mode of life for that day.

"Everything that we do should bear a relation to it; even if certain things should seem mutually exclusive, we must not avoid them, inasmuch as they form part of the whole of those things which go to make up realization.

"By being willing to sacrifice nothing we succeed too often in accomplishing nothing.

"We know the story of the man who one day found two robbers in his garden and set out to pursue them.

"He ran after them at first for a time, then at a fork of the road one of the two turned off to the right, while the other pursued his way.

"The man, undecided for a moment, rushed down the byroad, saying to himself that he would catch more easily the one that took the hard road, but after a time, out of breath, he perceived that he was not as quick as the robber, and bethought himself that the other was bigger and stouter and on that account easier to overtake.

"He, therefore, retraced his steps and rushed along the main road; but the man whom he was pursuing had had the time, in spite of his want of agility, to gain ground, and the pursuer puffed and blew in vain. He soon had the mortification of seeing him disappear, and his neighbors made fun of him."

How many times do we act likewise, without perceiving it, when we pursue two different ends and give them up, first one, then the other, according to the inclination of our idleness or of our whims?

Those who practice concentration will never commit this fault. They will never risk making themselves a laughing-stock like the people of whom Yoritomo speaks, for they will set out in pursuit of an undertaking only after reflecting deeply on the possibilities of success, and they will take every precaution against giving it up before they have brought it to a successful issue.

They who would be adequately prepared for this kind of reflection ought to bring themselves to it by the habitual contemplation of a thought. Our thoughts are tools, and the life substance is shaped with these tools. Every hour we can stand before our half-formed self and with tools a thousand times finer than those of the finest craftsman of the physical plane, we can cut, from our own thought atmosphere, forms of exquisite perfection, until body, environment, friends, even our whole life, is a world picture of peace, power, love, joy, health and wealth, limitless and

It is well to maintain the attention on the alert, and to keep oneself from every distraction by the repetition of one or several sayings bearing a relation to this thought, giving it concrete and definite form and persuading ourselves of the necessity of concentration.

Other methods also are employed with success; they make up those exercises that should be practiced by all those who wish to acquire any science, whatever it may be.

Of these methods, several were already known in the time of Yoritomo, and it is he who recommends us a procedure which he called "of the collar":

"Have," said he, "a collar containing about 200 beads of jade or of any other stone, if your means do not allow you to make use of jewels. Take care to string them not too close together in order to be able to take them off easily and make them slide slowly one over the other, counting ten between each bead.

"Your mind during this time should be occupied with only one thing: to allow between the beads the same space of time. Do not say the numbers too fast or too slowly, and do it in such a way, all the time that this exercise lasts, as to think thus regularly of nothing but *good*.

"When you find it impossible to keep up your thought, revive it as soon as you can and begin again.

"At first, it will be well not to extend the experiment farther than five or six beads.

"Afterward you can increase it, and some thinkers are mentioned who had such a mastery over their imaginations that they went right to the end of the beads without slackening."

With the same collar the Shogun shows us yet another exercise.

"You will take off," said he, "a handful of the beads (without counting them), in such a way that you are ignorant of the exact number, and, having fastened the collar together again, letting the place of joining be in sight, which will serve you as a starting-point, you will count aloud each bead that you take off with your finger-tip.

"That done, you will begin again three times—if you find the same number each time it means that your power of concentration has been sufficient to keep your attention without letting it wander.

"Where you find a different number, you should begin again until you obtain the same result three times in succession."

We might smile at the simplicity of these methods, nevertheless those who are devoted adepts in concentration know how difficult these results are to realize, if they wish to be sincere with themselves; before obtaining the same count of beads three times, they must often begin the experiment over again twenty times, for thought escapes easily when one can no longer keep it in subjection.

The Shogun recommends us yet other exercises:

"Sit down," said he, "comfortably on a seat soft enough to prevent your feeling any discomfort; this is very essential, for the least physical discomfort distracts the attention by directing it to the feeling of uneasiness which you experience.

"That done you will rest your hands on your breast, the palms well open, the fingers spread out.

"The left hand will be placed near the waist and the other near the throat; you will slowly pass the left hand down to the waist while you lift the other as far as the neck, taking great care, when the two hands meet, to touch lightly the tip of the middle finger of the left hand with the tip of the middle finger of the right hand.

"During the few minutes that this exercise lasts, you will do it in such a way as to think of nothing except the care of letting the fingers touch one another toward the middle of the breast, and in consequence of accelerating or retarding the movement in order to arrive at this result.

"During all this time force yourself to think of *nothing else.*"

This is what our modern philosophers recommend under the name of "devitalization."

Devitalization is the act of shutting oneself out from external impressions and moral sensations; it is a kind of arrest of thought, or rather of rupture of thought, which one concentrates on something so plainly commonplace that it gives birth to a sensible rest for us.

This is the first step, which leads to one of the most satisfactory forms of concentration *isolation*.

Without isolation, no meditation is possible, and consequently there is great difficulty in concentration.

Now we have just seen what part this faculty plays in training the mind.

It is that which allows us to rally our scattered psychical powers and to unite them on the same point, localizing them alone on the phases of the subject that engages our attention.

It is also recommended that we devote ourselves to the study of any object whatsoever and force ourselves to limit the effort of our thoughts to that object alone.

But this meditation may form the excuse for many mental vagaries.

One way of accomplishing this is to take a piece of paper and to concentrate our attention solely on the thought of this scrap; but is not this on the other hand a dangerous excuse for fancy to come into play?

Contemplate it: this piece of paper once formed part of some material. What material? Was it the white muslin of bridal veils'? Was it, on the other hand, the flimsy fabric in which a courtesan arrays herself? Whose hands tore it? In what religious processions or in what wretched dens was it used?

Later by what changes did it come to this condition of a scrap of paper?

Doubtless Yoritomo also believes this when he says:

"If you wish to devote yourself sincerely to the practice of concentration, guard yourself against allowing your thoughts to wander from the corolla to the stalk of the flower."

This means that one object alone, and that strictly limited, should engage our attention, if we wish to succeed in controlling our attention to the point at which it responds to our first call like an obedient servant.

Many feather-brained people think it a good excuse when they say: "It is not my fault, I forgot."

Not suspecting that forgetfulness is itself the fault with which they do not wish to be charged. It is an excuse glibly assigned by those whose moral infirmity is so evident that they are unable on their own account to make any effort worth the while.

It is the excuse of the weak and of people lacking courage.

It is a certificate of psychical incapacity awarded to those who have not in them the energy to practice self-recollection.

Meditation, which is closely allied to concentration, is a state of inward contemplation that allows us to shut ourselves in from external things so as to engage our thoughts solely on the subject that we have set before ourselves.

Many people over the centuries have practiced concentration by means of meditation. Some experts on meditation recommend that to concentrate, one should focus one's mind on a mantra, a sound that they will repeat over and over again during their period of meditation. Preferably it should be a sound that has no literal meaning, such as the humming sound "ommmmm." By repeating this mantra over and over, the mind is released from all other thoughts and it can concentrate on becoming totally relaxed.

Meditation gurus like the Maharishi Mahesh Yogi, who advocated the practice of transcendental meditation, a movement that became very popular in the mid-twentieth century, would personally give each of his followers their own mantra, a Sanskrit word that he felt fit that disciple's personality.

Some people prefer using a word or phrase that has special meaning for them. It may be a biblical text such as a brief proverb or part of a prayer. Some Catholics recite *Ave Maria*—some the entire prayer, some just the two-word title. Some select a specific thought that sets the stage for them. One woman reported that by just saying over and over *Today is the day*, she reinforced the principle that "yesterday is past and gone, tomorrow has not come, it is today that I must live now."

Select a mantra that best suits you. Incorporate this into your breathing exercises. Breathe in, repeat the mantra, as you breathe out—over and over again.

The difference between meditation and concentration lies in the greater freedom allowed to thought in the former state.

"Meditation," said Yoritomo, "is like a target of which concentration is the bull's-eye.

"Every arrow which hits the target has certainly attained its end, but those which quiver at it center are the only ones which, in ease of defense, would have sufficed to make our enemy bite the dust."

And he adds:

"Meditation is valuable above all because it is a rest; it is a kind of mental anesthesia which allows us to have faith in our liberty of thought, even when, nevertheless, we still confine it but less closely than in concentration.

"We could not devote ourselves to a fruitful meditation without being prepared for it by self-absorption.

"We must then allow ourselves to be slowly permeated by the idea which we wish to fathom and all the influences of which we wish to receive.

"But we ought to fear one redoubtable enemy—distraction. Nothing is more difficult for those who do not habitually practice this lesson than to meditate successfully, without letting the thoughts wander after ideas which are connected with one another but which end by reason of their number and diversity, by being completely removed from the initial point."

In fact, we have all experienced the impression of which the Shogun speaks; it has happened to all of us, after long periods of reflection, to find ourselves a hundred miles from the subject which we desired to conjure up, and when we wish to take account of the road traversed we find ourselves altogether amazed at the imperceptible concatenation of thoughts, which, without seeming to be foreign to the subject of our meditation, have drawn us in the direction of ideas completely dissimilar.

This is one of the familiar phases of distraction, that foe of concentration.

This is why Yoritomo puts us on our guard against pseudo-meditation, of which day-dreaming is, he says, the mischievous sister.

"Let us beware," says he, "of allowing ourselves to give way to day-dreaming, for thus we should contract the undesirable habit of allowing our attention to drowse; day-dreaming is a fabric on which fancy embroiders shapeless flowers, it scatters them without method or system at its own sweet will; these flowers are unreal and their colors soon fade.

"Day-dreaming is a dissipation of energy, it carries us away and we can not direct it.

"For this reason it is particularly dangerous, for it destroys our psychic forces and injures the development of strong mental powers."

It was with this in view, it is said, that a twelfth century Castillian friar, St. Dominic, invented the rosary.

He thought, like our Japanese philosopher, that meditation is so close akin to daydreaming that one should seek to control it by removing the temptations arising from the volatility of the imagination by means of a physical rallying of the idea.

The telling of the beads has no other object; all the decades end in a different prayer from the ten preceding it and, granting that the attention has wandered during the repetition of the ten "Hail Marys," the eleventh bead, separate from the others and appreciatively larger, comes to remind us of the change of the formula and brings back the most wandering minds to the subject of the meditation.

In short, such a director of souls as St. Dominic, knew well that daydreaming always possesses a pernicious charm which it is well to nip in the bud.

A great thinker, the eighteenth century French philosopher, Etienne Condillac, said further:

"Attention is like a light which is reflected from one body onto another, in order to illuminate both of them, and I call it reflection.

"... Sensible ideas represent to us the objects which actually impress themselves on our senses; intellectual ideas represent to us those which disappear after making their impression..."

He also said:

"Intellectual ideas, if they are familiar to us, recur to us at will."

This was also the teaching of Yoritomo who wrote:

"It suffices for those who practice concentration to *will* for the objects on which they wish to meditate to be recalled clearly before their eyes.

"Adepts in this art can, with very little effort and after placing themselves in a condition of self-absorption, transport themselves in imagination to the sphere where the phases of the occurrence which forms the subject of their thought unfold themselves before them.

"They will succeed in picturing to themselves places and persons in living movement, in so realistic a manner that they will even be sensible of the odors or the climate of the place that witnesses these happenings.

"What marvel that, finding themselves in this mental condition, it is easy for them to decide on sound resolutions and to thrust aside attempts to counsel for them a less studied decision?"

And he concludes:

"Those who would influence others should above all things know how to influence themselves in order to acquire the faculty of self-concentration which will allow of their reaching the highest degree of discernment.

"Many soothsayers have owed their influence over the multitude only to that spirit of concentrations that passed for prophecies.

"It is wrong and delusive to give credence to magic which is trickery, but we bear within us a power equal to that of the sorcerers whose deeds are related; this is the magic of the influence which prudent and self-possessed people always exercise over others, when their intentions are pure and when their ideals are nothing else than the amelioration of the condition of others, by the wholesome influence of their example and discourse."

Lesson XI
By Confidence

Confidence is the mental impulse that all those who wish to influence others should seek to elicit.

For most of them, it is the means of replacing the vacillating and ever faltering will with their own will, which they impose according to circumstances and according to the character of their followers.

With some, gentle persuasion is a means, even if slow, yet almost sure of success.

But we must guard the future adept from a diversity of influences, otherwise our minds will always retain the most recent impression, and before following the course of initiation we must give our attention to doing away with contradictory ideas that we cannot completely eradicate except with great difficulty.

This is one of the characteristics of feeble folk; their stubbornness has always to be combatted and we cannot succeed in teaching them confidence except after prolonged effort.

The best way left to us is not to hit them too hard, for their obstinacy—which they sometimes take for will-power—would form a troublesome obstacle to their conversion.

It is therefore better to seem to pay attention to their opinions, however baseless they may he, and to put before them objections that appear rather involuntary than otherwise and which to all appearances we regret the necessity of formulating.

This is what Yoritomo teaches us in the following anecdote:

"My master Lang-Ho," said he, "had among his disciples a chief who had great influence in the senate, not on account of his personal qualifications but rather of his wealth which was considerable.

"He had estates the extent of which gave him the privileges of a little king, and my master thought rightly that such a man should be gained over to the beauty of the Good, in order that his discourse should not be like the weeds of the field but on the contrary should resemble good seed the sprouting of which brings forth a whole course of bountiful harvest.

"But this nobleman suffered from a weakness of will that hindered him from profiting by any lesson.

"He would say 'yes' one day and the next day, after listening to the talk of those who had no other idea except to get money out of him, he would profess an opposite opinion and set himself obstinately to follow the most pernicious counsels.

"Lang-Ho, as I have already told you, was a profound psychologist; no recess of the human heart was hidden from him; so, after subjecting the chief to a lengthy scrutiny, he adopted the method which seemed likely to succeed.

"He did not dissuade him from acts which under evil influences this man had made up his mind to perform, but at first he, so to speak, channeled his infatuation toward things of less importance, the plan of which he seemed at first to entertain kindly.

"He was careful thus not to awaken the spirit of obstinacy which he knew was dormant in the chief's heart. But after putting him to the test and at the time when the latter was no longer in a suspicious mood, Lang-Ho enumerated to him the errors of his ways and did not fail to declare what mischief would accrue from them.

"This done, he let him follow his own devices or rather those of his evil counselors.

"This policy had the result of allowing the troubles which he had foretold to arise, so that by degrees the chief began to regard Lang-Ho with a kind of superstitious fear blended with a deep veneration.

"The philosopher waited no longer; he then took in hand the freeing of his disciple from his self-interested friends, and after some months of initiation the latter, imbued with the knowledge and wisdom of the master, ceased all resistance and gloried in showing to those who depended on him that he shared the opinions of the sage.

"From that to conversion was only one step, and that step was taken so successfully that, under the influence of Lang-Ho, the chief became a genuine benefactor to all who lived on his estates and who looked up to him as a master whose word has the force of an oracle."

But certain natures are restive under persuasion or two malleable for any impression to leave its marks on them.

In such, therefore, it is well to inspire confidence, somewhat in spite of themselves, by having recourse to suggestion.

All modern thinkers are of this opinion all those also who are engaged with mental infirmities.

We too readily give an idea of magic to the word suggestion. Suggestion, as the writer understands it, might be defined as follows: *The development of confidence.*

It is, in a way, the imposing of one's belief on the mind of others; it is not a quack method of enthralling people and of compelling them to carry out tasks which we feel ourselves but do not have the courage to perform; it is a noble faculty which choice spirits alone possess, that of implanting their belief in those whom they consider worthy of being persuaded.

Be it remembered that there is suggestion in everything; in the book which fascinates us and the theories of which gain possession of us in spite of ourselves; in the conversation to which we listen of our own accord, in the discussions of which only one side seems to us to express the truth.

But it happens too frequently that if afterward we recollect ourselves in order to judge our thoughts with the same impartiality, as we should those of others, we are altogether amazed to see the fine enthusiasm that had animated us fail; the principles of the book, stripped of the magic of style, seem to us highly debatable; the conversation which we enjoyed, when the illusion of eloquence no longer illumines it, seems to us insipid, and the object of discussion which had interested us deeply becomes a matter of indifference to us when we examine it calmly.

To what then is this sudden change to be ascribed?

Does it arise from ourselves? From our over-susceptibility to enthusiasm, or from our excessive propensity to fleeting impressions?

In most cases regarding these suggestions we should accuse only their authors, who, not being convinced themselves, have been unable to imbue us with a lasting confidence.

To inspire confidence without which no influence is possible, several qualities are indispensable:

Sincerity with ourselves;

Hatred of injustice;

Certainty in our decisions;

Absolute truth in our predictions;

Confidence in our own merits.

Sincerity with ourselves consists especially in the conviction of the necessity that exists of making others share in a belief the good effects of which we experience so deeply, that the failure to diffuse it abroad should seem to us a dereliction of all our duties.

You see why the appeal of missionaries is generally so powerful; the success of the apostolate is always subordinated to the sincerity of the convictions of those who expound them and to their certainty that they are performing a duty in inculcating them on those for whom they may prove a support and a consolation.

If speakers doubt their own statements, their voices will be less firm, the effulgence of their thoughts will less easily spread over the audience, and enthusiasm, the parent of absolute faith, will not lift them to carry them on their way.

But how different a reception will be accorded to the apostles who are themselves convinced. Let us listen to Yoritomo in this matter:

"Like a refreshing stream," said he, "the words of those who believe spread into the minds of their hearers and quench their thirst of moral support and lofty convictions.

"Like moths attracted by the light of tapers, they will all flock around those who are for them the light and know how to envelop them with its life-giving rays.

"As long as they speak, vistas of brightness are spread before them; if they vanish, they seem again to pass into darkness only brightened by the remembrance of the words of confidence and faith."

Those who know not hatred of injustice will never be able to exercise a salutary influence on others.

How could they attract to themselves confidence, the mother of conversion, if, by the unfairness of their judgments, they are subjected to that of others?

"No partiality," said Yoritomo, "should animate those who would win souls.

"It is by allowing themselves to fall into such lapses that they will lose all the authority which they would fain acquire.

"Strict justice alone should direct their words and preside over their acts.

"Where they are themselves quite in the dark and do not see on which side justice is ranged, they should refrain until the time when a close concentration permits them to see the situation clearly.

"If doubt continues, let them be very careful not to utter a decision the injustice of which events might demonstrate, thus weakening the trust which their disciples are pleased to place in them.

"It is more honorable to confess one's ignorance than to risk committing an injustice."

To secure certainty in our judgments, it is prudent sometimes to use artifice, like the sage of whose shrewdness Yoritomo tells us.

"It should never happen," said he, "that those who wish to inspire confidence should risk seeing it destroyed by an assertion that is not borne out by facts.

"In this matter it is wise to imitate the old philosopher Hong-Yi who would never say, 'That will happen,' but, 'you have acted in such a way as to bring on yourself such or such a misfortune,' or, 'you are acting with so much prudence as to deserve to be rewarded.'

"So that when events happened to confirm his learned forecasts, he did not fail to recall his sayings and his authority thereby increased more and more.

"It should be added that the events foreseen always came to pass, for the deductive powers of Hong-Yi were great and it was easy for him to presume the acts which his disciples might be expected to perform!"

But foreseeing and even prophesying are not sufficient to gain confidence and especially, to communicate it.

In order to implant it in the hearts of others, it is necessary to possess it—this splendid confidence in ourselves that works wonders.

Then it is that all those to whom thinking for themselves is a labor, those whose powers of resistance are fitful and ill-balanced, those whose moral idleness rises up against all individual initiative, will lift their heads and feel a new strength, relying on the feeling of confidence which they will experience first in the master and afterward in themselves.

The healing balm of faith will by its good qualities impregnate them in the gentlest fashion and, despising the faintheartedness that hitherto had marked their most trivial resolutions, they will advance fearlessly toward the goal that has become plainly visible to their sight.

It is a well-known fact that an imagined support often serves as well as the support itself.

We know the instance of toddlers who cannot bring themselves to walk without stumbling but who, as soon as we stretch out a finger to them, pretending thus to support them, steadies their steps in such a way that they can accomplish a walk of several yards without tottering.

If, however, we draw back the finger, which, as it seems to them, is the support that must guard them from falling, they advance a few steps with difficulty and cannot avoid tumbling down.

It is the same with timid souls; people who think they will die of fear in the solitude of an empty house will feel quite reassured if they imagine that the adjacent rooms are occupied.

The presence of others, creating a feeling of confidence in possible protection, suffices to save them from the fear which they would not fail to experience if they thought that in case of need there was no one to help them.

This protection, even when they know it to be illusory, suffices to allay their apprehensions.

Thus, although they are quite sure that they can expect nothing from the intervention of a child; timid persons almost always seek such company rather than remain alone, and they experience from it a real relief.

"Every impression," says Yoritomo, "which is not our own and which comes from outside is an influence which we perforce put up with.

"It is especially in cases of sickness that this influence can make its presence felt in the highest degree, for at such a time the subjects being very weak is best disposed to submit themselves to any suggestion whatsoever.

"There is a vague solidarity between mind and body which allows of the latter becoming as easy prey to affective conditions brought about by suffering.

"It would be idle to deny the connection between our physical ills and our mental sufferings.

"Some under the domination of weighty anxieties, become the victims of severe headache.

"Others again, after repeated emotional disturbances, contract heart troubles.

"It is therefore sometimes wiser to cure the mind before considering how to care for the body, or rather it is well to effect both cures at the same time.

"Now it is that influence makes itself felt, triumphant, radiant; it stamps on the nerve centers an impression which reverberates through one's whole being.

"Considering that our troubles are due to pain, to anxiety, to hypochondria, we should cultivate confidence and cheerfulness which take from our conceptions their somber coloring.

"If we have been able to inspire invalids with confidence, we shall be glad to tell them that they are getting better, for they will not doubt the truth of the assertion and that assurance will cause them to experience a real improvement.

"Miracles have no other basis than this."

And the Shogun proceeds:

"But the grandest means of effecting these cures is to implant in the mind of self-imagined invalids the idea of devotion to a noble cause; to plunge them into a tide of ambition that will make them gradually forget their everlasting 'Ego.' For this over-coddled 'Ego' is the real cause of most of these disorders from which all persons suffer whom a surfeit of 'Ego' so dominates that their most trivial ailments command their whole attention and seem to them to be entitled to command that of everybody else to the exclusion of all other things.

"On such influence should be exercised in quite different a manner.

"It will suffice to create about them an atmosphere of activity in which their personality will play a dominating part; they will thus forget to spend their time in looking out for the attacks of an illness which exists only in their own brain, and those who assists them to a cure may congratulate themselves doubly, for they will have made their beneficial influence felt in the case of both mind and body.

"Assuredly the best of suggestions is that which lies in, as it were, devitalizing the self-centered person, by substituting for the worshiper of his or her 'Ego' an altruist who, thoroughly imbued with faith in him or herself and strong in the mission with which that person truly believes, will seek to impart to others the benefits of that confidence from which that person has derived so much consolation."

Thus will the advice of Yoritomo be proved right when he says:

"Let those who feel themselves to be in the right and have Confidence in themselves rise up and proclaim this faith, so that the weak, the vacillating, and all those who suffer from doubt may flock around them to warm themselves at the genial blaze that issues from the fire of contentment of which their minds are full."

Lesson XII
Acquisition of Dominating Power

"The warriors of old," said Yoritomo, "were very fond of insignia, which they believed to be likely to impress their enemies.

"They liked to wear fearsome masks, the manes of beasts, or helmets the top of which represented the head of an animal.

"One great general arrayed himself in a helmet the tip of which bore the figure of a mattock (a digging tool in which the blade is perpendicular to the handle—used as a combined pick and shovel) and on the visor were engraven characters the combination of which represented the words 'mattock,' 'way,' and 'rock,' which the learned have interpreted as follows: "If the 'way' is not opened by my 'mattock,' I will lay it out even in the 'rock.'

"Now what idea dominated all those warriors if not the desire to impress their enemies, some by fear, others by intimidation?

"But there is a kind of influence a thousand fold more valuable than all these rude methods and barbarous attempts to bring about an emotion by means of bloodthirsty symbols.

"The domain of thought is open to all those who feel themselves worthy of entering it; it is for those who know the turnings of a beautiful garden with multifarious paths.

"On each fresh excursion they discover some hitherto unknown paths which they explore always with increasing interest.

"The flowers which border them are gorgeous or poor, according as they shed on them the rays of intelligence placed at the disposal of the powers of the will which are latent in them.

"But those whose languid action can not lift he torch, whose indolence neglects to enkindle do not enjoy the sight of these diversified flowers.

"In the gloom from which they look on them, they perceive them but indistinctly, and the path seems to them so uninteresting that they lose the desire to seek in it for new objects.

"Those, on the other hand, who know how to throw the floral beauties into the light derive from their contemplation so exquisite an enjoyment that there always arises in them the desire for fresh explorations, and also the wish to share their admiration, by introducing some persons to the marvels which they have encountered, and by teaching others how to see them in all their splendor.

"This is the secret of the dominating influence which certain people exercise over others.

"Those alone who know how to throw the flowers of thought into the light, after having sought and found them, can acquire sufficient power to influence the destinies of others."

This is what, in language less florid but nonetheless ornate, modern thinkers tell us:

"There is an intercommunication between ourselves and others of such a nature that perpetually, night and day, we are receiving and giving forth again influences which model us, change us, and gradually alter our mode of life.

"It is, therefore, through instigation from without that we end by making ourselves what we are: good or bad, happy or miserable."

"Thought plays a decisive part in human life. It encompasses the individual. It is the cord which binds us to others and by means of which are gathered together, to join and mingle in a single current, all surrounding energies."

It is a method of acquiring the power necessary to first subdue those whom we wish afterward to influence:

"By causing mental currents to pass from you too the other parties under the form of timely questions and suggestions, you awaken in them responsive currents; you find out their likes and dislikes, and, by encouraging their confidence, through the current derived from an approval delicately expressed, you will soon succeed in making them vibrate in unison with yourself."

Those who would acquire the power of domination over the minds of those they wish to direct must, above all, compel themselves to create between them and their disciple a kind of intellectual level which will be of infinite service to those people.

It is by creating empathy that these vibrations in unison, so indispensable in the formation of influence, will be obtained.

Empathy—the art of truly understanding another by "putting oneself in that person's shoes"—begets confidence and paves the way for beneficent suggestion.

"Those who know how to attract empathy," said Yoritomo, "is like a kindly light toward which turn all those whose minds are covered with moral darkness.

"Their development is rarely very speedy, and that is preferable, otherwise they would be dazzled before being enlightened; it is better to attract them slowly but irresistibly.

"Then, already imbued with the distant radiance, they will already have come out of darkness when they approach quite near to those who are to give them clear light and, grown familiar with the brilliant rays, they will endure its utmost intensity without flinching."

It is, in fact, one of the powers of empathy to attract slowly but to retain surely those who feel themselves drawn to an empathetic person by an attraction at first vague and ill-defined later justified by a thousand reasons, the principal of which, and soon the only one, will be the attraction which those who possess dominating power exert over others.

It is better, as Yoritomo says, for this power to assert itself less roughly to have more chances of permanency.

It is preferable to illumine slowly people's minds with a well-defined gleam than to dazzle them to the extent of causing them a discomfort, which will make them seek the darkness as a relief.

One of the secrets of dominating power lies in exciting similarity of feelings by adopting for the time being those, which are within the compass of those whom we wish to influence.

The feeling of condescension should be given up by strong minds. Those who believe that they are lowering themselves with regard to their disciples, by instilling in them principles which they regard as too elementary, will never succeed as a leader.

Those who would use the power of suggestion in earnest should for a moment give up their own minds to adopt that of the persons they are teaching. This is the only way of creating a bond of mutual confidence.

"Those who would teach the first characters in writing should be able to create a child's mind in themselves," said the Shogun.

We must admit that, to fulfill this condition, it is necessary to be already in possession of a rare self-mastery.

Only those who can master themselves are qualified to master others.

If ambition and confidence in one's own worth are the attributes of dominating power, self-sufficiency is always the stumbling block over which one trips whom pride prevents from looking down at one's own feet.

Self-sufficiency almost always begets arrogance, which is of no use for producing empathy and confidence.

This exaggerated idea of "Ego" is never dictated by the consciousness of real merit, but rather by the imaginary swelling of virtues that we ascribe too freely to ourselves, as though to divert our minds with the noise of our own words.

If we wish to be sincere, we shall recognize very quickly that these virtues are imaginary, and that the parade that we make of them arises only from a great desire to possess them; but, the power having failed for assuring the gaining of them, we prefer, by proclaiming loudly that we possess them, to shirk the effort of acquiring them.

This is why egotistical, smug persons, in the category of whom we must place those out of whom an empty pride beats out nobility of character, will never have the aptitude for exerting an influence over the minds of others.

Unable to derive from themselves the energy necessary to become what they would like to be, they cannot emit around themselves that power which fails them, and their domination over others will never be established.

Melancholy persons, those who are the victims of hypochondria, are by no means destined to become shepherds of the multitude.

Melancholy almost always begets a mental condition bordering on indifference; it suppresses the desire for life, the key of all good resolutions and continual perseverance.

Every effort of the melancholy is quickly halted by that terrible thought, "What is the good?" which proclaims the end of everything and the vanity of life.

What influence can people exercise if their powers of energy are destroyed by indifference and apathy?

They have hardly the strength to live themselves; where will they find the strength to teach others?

Cheerfulness is one of the requisite conditions for controlling others; not that boisterous mirth which is made up of bursts of laughter, the reasons for which are not always of the most refined nature, but that inward peace which we define as cheerfulness and which is the mark of highly developed minds.

People of fine character will never be melancholy. Hypochondria is the trade-mark of the incapable; it is the commencement of manias and of all crazes that desolate humanity and abase its moral level.

The philosophers of ill omen whose teaching has clouded so many young brains have defined enjoyment as follows: "Cessation of suffering."

Ah, well! But is not that worth an effort, to suffer no longer, and can we regard as a madman the people who labor to end this suffering, by substituting for it the joy of living, which opens minds to the cult of beauty?

The art of happiness lies especially in the great wish to live.

If Yoritomo was not willing to raise the burning question of free will, he nonetheless admits the unquestionable influence of each one of us on our own destiny.

"We," said he, "are for the most part like the fool who shivered, cowering in a snowdrift, while around him the sun bathed the mountain with its burning rays.

"He cursed the snow, the cold, the hateful country where he dwelt, and the misery of his existence which had to be spent in suffering and barrenness.

"In vain people signaled to him of nearby paths, in vain they showed him from afar flowers gathered on the way; he was obstinately bent on doing nothing to free himself from his sufferings and continued to curse the place which it would have been so easy to leave and deplored the unhappiness of the fate which had caused him to be born in that inclement country."

Have we not here in very truth the picture of the pessimist who denies the existence of happiness and beauty while pretending to turn away when they pass?

Such persons may perchance exercise a pernicious influence over weak minds, but it will always be limited, for—we cannot repeat it too often—real influence over others is only acquired at the price of complete mastery of oneself.

This mastery should be the aim of the efforts of those who wish to possess this faculty and to make use of it for their own happiness and that of those with whom they come in contact.

"Again," said the Nippon philosopher, "we should keep ourselves from too commonplace associations, for, granting this truth that the thought which we emit about us is taken in by those around, we ought to beware of the imbibing of commonplace thought which, when repeated too often, will end by occupying, unknown to ourselves, a place in our brain and will weaken the quality of the power.

"The higher type person should never harbor a medley of ideas.

"Those who frame, the waves of which spread themselves around them, succeed by a succession of undulating movements which may be compared with those of sound, in striking the intelligence of others by setting their brains in vibration, in other words, in a state to receive the floating thought.

"But the really forceful people, those whose secret energies are concentrated on the gaining of influence, those who aim to acquire dominating power, will harbor no ignoble thoughts, for they will not barter away the first to arrive of these flowers of the mind; if they find themselves among people of small intellectual caliber, they will surpass them with all the mighty power that their knowledge and strength of will confer.

"They will know how to listen to other people, then to talk to them, perhaps to convince them, but not for a moment will they submit themselves to imbibing their commonplace thoughts. For having come among them in as apostles they are conscious of their own excellence. They know too well their own superiority They are, in a word, on too lofty a pedestal to allow themselves to be affected by things beneath them.

"Does the granite stoop to the ivy that twines itself about it while mounting toward the towers in its need of protection and support?"

The Shogun remarks also that this plant, which, without the support of the granite, would trail miserably on the ground, ends, when it has covered the surface at every point, by forming an essential part of the building, to such a degree that its frail tendrils effect more for the durability of the works of man than the hardest marbles chiseled by the most skillful artisans.

And he adds:

"How many ancient towers, that seemed of unquestionable solidity, crumble to pieces when deprived of the parasites that seemed to overrun them?

"So it is with all those who possess power; they maintain themselves only because they create disciples whose devotion serves to consolidate their work.

"But if they can not retain the influence, which at first they had sent forth around them, their followers fall away one by one, and they, left alone, soon see the edifice of their superiority crumble to pieces."

"Dominating power," Yoritomo proceeds, "is developed especially by an apostolate the exercise of which, by creating a mental current between the masters and those whom they are teaching, wards off opposing currents."

In the cant of modern science it is said in fact that material builders, drawn by the attractive force of thought, are always displaced in feeble minds by a stronger influence, bit that the converse does not hold good.

Such is the comment of the Japanese philosopher when he tells us:

"Do not rub shoulders with a commonplace mind except with the intention of raising that person to your own level, but do not think of entering in mental communion with such before making it worthy of it."

This luminous sentence may serve as a commentary on Yoritomo's entire teaching, for every line of his writings is an appeal to energy, an invitation to the practice of the cult of moral beauty, and an encouragement to that advance toward the better, which should guide our steps toward the enchanted temple on the façade of which are emblazoned these eternal words: *Truth, Courage,* and *Cheerfulness.*

BOOK 2
Common Sense: How to Exercise It

Contents

Foreword to the Original Edition   147
Introduction by Editor of Original Edition   149

Lesson I
Common Sense: What Is It?   151

Lesson II
The Fight Against Illusion   163

Lesson III
The Development of the Reasoning Power   172

Lesson IV
Common Sense and Impulse   183

Lesson V
The Dangers of Sentimentality   193

Lesson VI
The Utility of Common Sense   202

Lesson VII
Power of Deduction   211

Lesson VIII
How to Acquire Common Sense   221

Lesson IX
Common Sense and Action   234

Lesson X
The Most Thorough Business Manager   242

Lesson XI
Common Sense and Self-Control   252

Lesson XII
Common Sense Does Not Exclude Great Aspirations   260

Foreword to Original Edition

The quality popularly designated as "Common Sense" comprehends, according to the modern point of view, the sound judgment of humankind when reflecting upon problems of truth and conduct without bias from logical subtleties or selfish interests. It is one of Nature's priceless gifts; an income in itself, it is as valuable as its application is rare.

How often we hear the expression "Why, I never thought of that!" *Why?* Because we have failed to exercise Common Sense—that genius of humankind, which when properly directed is the one attribute that will carry us successfully through the perplexities of life. Common Sense is as a plant of delicate growth, in need of careful training and continued watching so that it may bear fruit at all seasons. In the teachings that follow, the venerable Shogun, Yoritomo-Tashi, points out that Common Sense is a composite product consisting of (1) Perception; (2) Memory; (3) Thought; (4) Alertness; (5) Deduction; (6) Foresight; (7) Reason, and (8) Judgment. Discussing each of these separately, he indicates their relations and how they may be successfully employed. Further, he warns one against the dangers that lurk in moral inertia, indifference, sentimentality, egotism, etc.

Common Sense is a quality that must be developed if it is to be utilized to the full of its practical value. Indispensable to this development are such qualifications—(1) Ability to grasp situations; (2) Ability to concentrate the mind; (3) Keenness of perception; (4) Exercise of the reasoning power; (5) Power of approximation; (6) Calmness; (7) Self-control, etc. Once mastered, these qualifications enable one to reap the reward of a fine and an exalted sense, and of a practical common sense which sees things as they are and does things as they should be done.

The desire for knowledge, like the thirst for wealth, increases by acquisition, but knowledge without common sense is folly; without method it is waste; without kindness it is fanaticism; without religion it is death. With common sense, it is wisdom; with method it is power; with charity beneficence; and with religion it is virtue, life, and peace.

In these pages, Yoritomo-Tashi teaches his readers how to overcome such defects of the understanding as may beset them. He shows them how to acquire and develop Common Sense and practical sense, how to apply them in their daily lives, and how to utilize them profitably in the business world.

To him Common Sense is the crown of all faculties. Exercised vigilantly, it leads to progress and prosperity, therefore, he says "Enthusiasm is as brittle as crystal, but Common Sense is durable as brass."

Introduction
by B. Dangennes, Editor of Original Edition

Why should I hesitate to express the pleasure I felt on learning that the public, already deeply interested in the teachings of Yoritomo-Tashi, desired to be made familiar with them in a new form?

This knowledge meant many interesting and pleasant hours of work in prospect for me, recalling the time passed in an atmosphere of that peace which gives birth to vibrations of healthful thoughts whose radiance vitalizes the soul.

It was also with a zeal, intensified by memories of the little deserted room in the provincial museum, where silence alone could lend rhythm to meditation, that I turned over again and again the leaves of those precious manuscripts, translating the opinions of him whose keen and ornate psychology we have so often enjoyed together.

It was with the enthusiastic attention of the disciple that once more I scanned the pages, where the broadest and most humane compassion allies itself with those splendid virtues: Energy—Will—Reason.

For altho Yoritomo glorifies the Will and Energy under all their aspects, he knows also how to find, in his heart, that tenderness which transforms these forces, occasionally somewhat brutal, into powers for good, whose presence are always an indication of favorable results.

He knows how to clothe his teachings in fable and appealing legend, and his exotic soul, so near and yet so far, reminds one of a flower, whose familiar aspect is transmuted into rare perfume.

By him the sternest questions are stript of their hostile aspects and present themselves in the alluring form of the simplest allegories of striking poetic intensity.

When reading his works, one recalls unconsciously the orations of the ancient philosophers, delivered in those dazzling gardens, luxuriant in sunlight and fragrant with flowers.

In this far-away past, one sees also the silhouette of a majestic figure, whose school of philosophy became a religion, which interested the world because it spoke both of love and goodness.

But in spite of this fact, the doctrines of Yoritomo are of an imaginative type.

His kingdom belongs to this world, and his theories seek less the joys of the hereafter than of that tangible happiness which is found in the realization of the manly virtues and in that effort to create perfect harmony from which flows perfect peace.

He takes us by the hand, in order to lead us to the center of that Eden of Knowledge where we have already discovered the art of persuasion, and that art, most difficult of all to acquire—the mastery of timidity.

Following him, we shall penetrate once more this Eden, that we may study with Yoritomo the manner of acquiring this art—somewhat unattractive perhaps but essentially primordial—called Common Sense.

Lesson I

Common Sense: What Is It?

One beautiful evening Yoritomo-Tashi was strolling in the gardens of his master, Lang-Ho, listening to the wise counsels which he knew so well how to give in all attractiveness of allegory, when, suddenly, he paused to describe a part of the land where the gardener's industry was less apparent.

Here parasitic plants had, by means of their tendrils, crept up the shrubbery and stifled the greater part of its flowers.

Only a few of them reached the center of the crowded bunch of the grain stalks and of the trailing vines that interlaced the tiny bands that held them against the wall.

One plant alone, of somber blossom and rough leaves, was able to flourish even in close proximity to the wild verdure; it seemed that this plant had succeeded in avoiding the dangerous entanglements of the poisonous plants because of its tenacious and fearless qualities, at the same time its shadow was not welcome to the useless and noxious creeping plants.

"Behold, my son," said the Sage, "and learn how to understand the teachings of nature. The parasitic plants represent negligence against the force of which the best of intentions vanish.

"Energy, however, succeeds in overcoming these obstacles that increase daily; it marks out its course among entanglements and rises from the midst of the most encumbered centers, beautiful and strong.

"Ambition and audacity show themselves also after having passed through thousands of difficulties and having overcome them all.

"Common sense rarely needs to strive; it unfolds itself in an atmosphere of peace, far from the tumult of obstructions and snares that are not easily avoided.

"Its flower is less alluring than many others, but it never allows itself to be completely hidden through the wild growth of neighboring branches.

"It dominates them easily, because it has always kept them at a distance.

"Modest but self-sustaining, it is seen blossoming far from the struggles which always retard the blossoming of plants and which render their flowering slower and, at times, short-lived."

A most absurd prejudice has occasionally considered common sense to be an, inferior quality of mind.

This error arises from the fact that it can adapt itself as well to the most elevated conceptions as to the most elemental mentalities.

To those who possess common sense is given the faculty of placing everything in its proper rank.

It does not underestimate the value of sentiments by attributing to them an exaggerated importance.

It permits us to consider fictitious reasons with reservation and of resolutely rejecting those that resort to the weapons of hypocrisy.

Persons who cultivate common sense never refuse to admit their errors.

One may truly affirm that they are rarely far from the truth, because they practice directness of thought and force themselves never to deviate from this mental attitude.

COMMON SENSE: HOW TO EXERCISE IT

Abandoning for a moment his favorite demonstration by means of symbolism, Yoritomo said to us:

"Common sense should be thus defined:

"It is a central sense, toward which all impressions converge and unite in one sentiment—the desire for the truth.

"For people who possess common sense, everything is summed up in one unique perception:

"The love of directness and simplicity.

"All thoughts are found to be related; the preponderance of these two sentiments makes itself felt in all resolutions, and chiefly in the reflections which determine them.

"Common sense permits us to elude fear which always seizes those whose judgment vacillates; it removes the defiance of the Will and indicates infallibly the correct attitude to assume."

And Yoritomo, whose mind delighted in extending his observations to the sociological side of the question, adds:

"Common sense varies in its character, according to surroundings and education.

"The common sense of one class of people is not the same as that of a neighboring class.

"Certain customs, which seem perfectly natural to Japan would offend those belonging to the western world, just as our Nippon prejudices would find themselves ill at ease among certain habits customary among Europeans."

"Common sense," he continues, "takes good care not to assail violently those beliefs which tradition has transmuted into principles.

"However, if direct criticism of those beliefs causes common sense to be regarded unfavorably, it will be welcomed with the greatest reserve and will maintain a certain prudence relative to this criticism, which will be equivalent to a proffered reproach.

"Common sense often varies as to external aspects, dependent upon education, for it is evident that a *diamio* (Japanese prince) can not judge a subject in the same way as would a person belonging to the lowest class of society.

"The same object can become desirable or undesirable according to the rank it occupies.

"Must one believe that common sense is excluded from two such incompatible opinions?

"No, not at all; an idea can be rejected or accepted by common sense without violating the principles of logic in the least.

"If, as one frequently sees, an idea be unacceptable because of having been presented before those belonging to a particular environment, common sense, by applying its laws, will recognize that the point of view must be changed before the idea can become acceptable."

Yoritomo calls our attention to a peculiar circumstance.

"Common sense," he says, "is the art of resolving questions, not the art of posing them.

"When taking the initiative it is rarely on trial.

"But the moment it is a case of applying practically that which ingenuity, science or genius have invented, it intervenes in the happiest and most decisive manner.

"Common sense is the principle element of discernment.

"Therefore, without this quality, it is impossible to judge either of the proposition or the importance of the subject.

"It is only with the aid of common sense that it is possible to distinguish the exact nature of the proposition, submitted for a just appreciation, and to render a solution of it which conforms to perfect accuracy of interpretation.

"The last point is essential and has its judicial function in all the circumstances of life. Without accuracy, common sense cannot be satisfactorily developed, because it finds itself continually shocked by incoherency, resulting from a lack of exactness in the expression of opinions."

If we wish to know what the principal qualities are which form common sense, we shall turn over a few pages and we shall read:

"Common sense is the synthesis of many sentiments, all of which converge in forming it.

"The first of these sentiments *is reason*.

"Then follows *moderation*.

"To these one may add;

"The faculty of *penetration;*

"The quality of *consistency.*

"Then, add *wisdom,* which permits us to profit by the lessons of experience.

"A number of other qualities must be added to these, in order to complete the formation of common sense; but, although important, they are only the satellites of those we have just named.

"Reason is really indispensable to the projection of healthy thoughts.

"The method of reasoning should be the exhaustive study of minute detail, of which we shall speak later.

"For the moment we shall content ourselves by indicating, along the broad lines of argument, what is meant by this word *reason*.

"Reasoning is the art of fixing the relativeness of things.

"It is by means of reasoning that it is possible to differentiate events and to indicate to what category they belong.

"It is the habit of reasoning to determine that which it is wise to undertake, thus permitting us to judge what should be set aside.

"How could we guide ourselves through life without the beacon-light of reason? It pierces the darkness of social ignorance, it helps us to distinguish vaguely objects heretofore plunged in obscurity, and which will always remain invisible to those who are not provided with this indispensable accessory—the gift of reasoning.

"Those who venture in the darkness and walk haphazardly, find themselves suddenly confronted by obstacles that they were unable to foresee.

"They find themselves frightened by forms whose nature they cannot define, and are often tempted, to attribute silhouettes of assassins to branches of trees, instead of recognizing the real culprits who are watching them from the corner of the wild forest.

"Life, as well as the wildest wilderness, is strewn with pitfalls. To think of examining it rapidly, without the aid of that torch called reason, would be imitating the people of whom we have just spoken.

"Many are the mirages, which lead us to mistake dim shadows for disquieting realities, unless we examine them critically, for otherwise we can never ascribe to them their true value.

"Certain incidents, which seem at first sight to be of small importance, assume a primordial value when we have explained them by means of reasoning.

"To reason about a thing is to dissect it, to examine it from every point of view before adopting it, before deferring to it or before rejecting it; in one word, to reason about a thing is to act with conscious volition, which is one of the phases essential to the conquest of common sense.

"This principle conceded, it then becomes a question of seriously studying the *method of* reasoning, which we propose to do in the following manner but first it is necessary to be convinced of this truth."

Without reason there is no common sense.

Yoritomo teaches us that, although moderation is only of secondary importance, it is still indispensable to the attainment of common sense.

It is moderation, which incites us to restrain our impatience, to silence our inexplicable antipathies and to put a break on our tempestuous enthusiasms.

Can one judge of the aspect of a garden while the tempest is twisting the branches of the trees, tearing off the tendrils of the climbing vines, scattering the petals of the flowers and spoiling the corollas already in full bloom?

And now, Yoritomo, who loves to illustrate his teachings by expressive figures of speech, tells us the following story:

"A Japanese prince, on awakening, one day, demanded lazily of his servants what kind of weather it was, but he forbade them to raise the awnings which kept a cool, dim light in his room and shielded his eyes from the strong light from without. The two servants left him reclining upon his divan and went into the adjoining room, where the stained-glass windows were not hung with curtains.

"One of them, putting his face close to a yellow-tinted pane of glass, exclaimed in admiration of the beautiful garden, bathed in the early morning sunlight.

"The second one, directing his gaze to a dark blue pane and, looking through the center, remarked to his companion, I see no sunshine, the day is dreary and the clouds cast gloomy shadows upon the horizon.

"Each one returned to relate their impressions of the weather, and the prince wondered at the different visions, unable to understand the reason."

There, concluded the Shogun is what happens to people who do not practice moderation.

Those, who see things through the medium of enthusiasm, refuse to recognize that they could be deprived of brilliancy and beauty.

The others, those who look upon things from a pessimistic standpoint, never find anything in them save pretexts for pouring out to their hearers' tales of woe and misery.

All find themselves deceptively allured; some rush toward illusion, others do not wish to admit the positive chances for success, and both lacking moderation, they start from a basis of false premises from which they draw deplorable conclusions, thus defeating future success.

The spirit of penetration, according to the old Nippon philosopher, is not always a natural gift. "It is," said he, "a quality which certain people possess in a very high degree but which in spite this fact should be strengthened by will and discipline.

"One can easily acquire this faculty by endeavoring to foresee the solution of contemporary events; or at least try to explain the hidden reasons which have produced them.

"Great effects are produced, many times, from seemingly unimportant causes, and it is, above all, to the significant details that the spirit of penetration should give unceasing and undivided attention.

"Everything around us can serve as a subject for careful study; political events, incidents which interest family or friends, all may serve as just so many themes for earnest reflection.

"It is always preferable to confine this analysis to subjects in which we have no personal interest; thus we shall accustom ourselves to judge of people and things dispassionately and impersonally. This is the quality of mind necessary to the perfect development of penetration.

"If, for any reason, passion should create confusion of ideas, clearness of understanding would be seriously compromised and firmness of judgment, by deteriorating, would cast aside the manifestation of common sense.

"The spirit consistency is perhaps more difficult to conquer, for it is a combination of many of the qualities previously mentioned.

"Its inspiration is drawn from the reasoning faculty; it cannot exist without moderation and implies a certain amount of penetration, because it must act under the authority of conviction.

"If you strike long enough in the same place on the thickest piece of iron, in time it will become as thin as the most delicate *kakemono* [a picture which hangs in Japanese homes].

"It is impossible to define the spirit of consistency more accurately.

"It is closely related to perseverance, but can not be confounded with it, because the attributes of consistency have their origin in logic and reason which does not produce one act alone but a series of acts sometimes dependent, always inferred.

"The spirit of consistency banishes all thought derogatory to the subject in question; it is the complete investiture of sentiments, all converging toward a unique purpose."

This purpose can be of very great importance and the means of attainment multiform, but the dominant idea will always direct the continuous achievements; under their different manifestations—and these at times contradictory—they will never be other than the emanation of a direct thought, whose superior authority is closely united to the final success.

Wisdom, continued the philosopher, should be mentioned here only as the forerunner which permits us to analyze experience.

It is from this never-ending lesson which life teaches us that the wisdom of old age is learned.

But is it really necessary to reach the point of decrepitude, in order to profit by an experience, actually useless at that time, as is always a posthumous conquest.

"Is it not much better to compel its attainment when the hair is black and the heart capable of hope?

"Why give to old age alone the privileges of wisdom and experience?

"It is high time to combat so profound an error.

"Is it not a cruel irony that renders such a gift useless?

"Of what benefit is wisdom resulting from experience if it can not preserve us from the unfortunate seduction of youth?

"Why should its beauty be unveiled only to those who can no longer profit by it?" This is the opinion of Yoritomo, who says:

"What would be thought of one who prided himself on possessing bracelets when he had lost his two arms in war?

"It is, therefore, necessary, not only to encourage young people to profit by lessons of wisdom and experience, but, still further, to indicate to them how they can accomplish the result of these lessons.

"It is certain that those who can recall a long life ought to understand better than the young all the pitfalls with which it is strewn.

"But do they always judge of it without bias or prejudice?

"Do they not find acceptable pretexts for excusing their past faults and do they not exaggerate the rewards for excellence, which have accorded them advantages, due at times to chance or to the force of circumstances?

"Finally, older people can not judge of the sentiments which they held at twenty years of age, unless it be by the aid of reminiscences, more or less fleeting, and an infinitely attenuated intensity of representation.

"Emotive perception being very much weakened, the integrity of memory must be less exact.

"Then, in the recession of years, some details, which were at times factors of the initial idea, are less vivid, thus weakening the power of reason which was the excuse, the pretext, or the origin of the act.

"This is why, although we may honor the wisdom of the aged, it is well to acquire it at a time when we may use it as a precious aid.

"To those who insist that nothing is equivalent to personal experience, we shall renew our argument, begging them to meditate on the preceding lines, drawing their attention to the fact that a just opinion can only be formed when personal sentiment is excluded from the discussion.

"Is it, then, necessary to have experienced pain in order to prevent or cure it?

"The majority of physicians have never suffered the diseases they treat.

"Does this fact prevent them from combating disease victoriously?

"And since we are speaking of common sense we shall not hesitate to invoke it in this instance, and all will agree that it should dictate our reply.

"Then why could we not do for the soul that which can be done for the body?

"It is first from books, then from the lessons of life that physicians learn the principles underlying their knowledge of disease and its healing remedies.

"Is it absolutely indispensable for us to poison ourselves in order to know that such and such a plant is harmful and that another contains the healing substance which destroys the effects of the poison?

"We may all possess wisdom if we are willing to be persuaded that the experience of others is as useful as our own."

The events which multiply about us, Yoritomo says, ought to be, for each master, an opportunity for awakening in the soul of his disciples a perfect reasoning power, starting from the inception of the premises to arrive at the conclusions of all arguments.

From the repetition of events, from their co-relation, from their equivalence, from their parallelism, knowledge will be derived and will be productive of good results, in proportion as egotistical sentiment is eliminated from them; and slowly, with the wisdom acquired by experience, common sense will manifest itself tranquil and redoubtable, working always for the accomplishment of good as does everything which is the emblem of strength and peace.

Lesson II
The Fight Against Illusion

Common Sense such as we have just described it, according to Yoritomo, is the absolute antithesis of dreamy imagination; it is the sworn enemy of illusion, against which it struggles from the moment of contact.

Common sense is solid; illusion is yielding. Illusion never issues victorious from a combat with it; during a struggle illusion endeavors vainly to display its subterfuges and cunning; illusions disappear one by one, crushed by the powerful arms of their terrible adversary—common sense.

"The worship of illusion," says Yoritomo, "presents certain dangers to the integrity of judgment, which, under such influence, falsifies the comparative faculty, and sways decision to the side of neutrality.

"This kind of mental half-sleep is extremely detrimental to manifestations of reason, because this torpor excludes it from imaginary conceptions.

"Little by little the lethargy caused by this intellectual paralysis produces the effect of fluidic contagion over all our faculties.

"Energy, which ought to be the principle factor in our resolutions, becomes feeble and powerless at the point where we no longer care to feel its influence.

"The sentiment of effort exists no longer, since we are pleased to resolve all difficulties without it.

"In this inconstant state of mind, common sense, after wandering a moment withdraws itself, and we find that we are delivered over to all the perils of imagination.

"Nothing that we see thus confusedly is found on the plane which belongs to common sense; the ideas, associated by a capricious tie, bind and unbind themselves, without imposing the necessity of a solution.

"People who allow themselves to be influenced by vague dreams," adds the Shogun, "must, if they do not react powerfully, bid farewell to common sense and reason; for they will experience so great a charm in forgetting, even for one moment, the reality of life, that they will seek to prolong this blessed moment.

"They will renounce logic, whose conclusions are, at times, opposed to their desires, and they will plunge themselves into that false delight of awakened dreams, or, as some say, day-dreams.

"Those who defend this artificial conception of happiness, like to compare people of common sense to heavy infantry soldiers, who march along through stony roads, while they depict themselves as pleasant bird-fanciers, giving flight to the fantastic bearers of wings.

"But they do not take into account the fact that the birds, for whom they open the cage, fly away without the intention of returning, leaving them thus deceived and deprived of the birds, while the rough infantry soldiers, after many hardships, reach the desired end which they had proposed to attain, thus realizing the joys of conquest.

"There they find the rest and security, which the possessors of fugitive birds will never know.

"Those who cultivate common sense will always ignore the collapses that follow the disappearance of illusions.

"How many people have suffered thus uselessly! And what is more stupid than a sorrow, voluntarily imposed, when it cannot be productive of any good?

"People can not be too strongly warned against the tendency of embellishing everything that concerns the heart-life, and this is the inclination of most people.

"The causes of this propensity are many and the need for that which astounds is not the only cause to be mentioned.

"Indolence is never a stranger to illusion.

"It is so delightful to foresee a solution that conforms to our desires!

"For certain natures, stained with moral atrophy, it is far sweeter to hope for that which will be produced without pain.

"One begins by accelerating this achievement, so earnestly desired, by using all the will-power, and one becomes accustomed progressively to regard desires as a reality, and, aided by indolence, discounts in advance an easy success.

"False enthusiasm, or rather enthusiasm without deliberate reflection, always enters into these illusions, which are accompanied by persuasion and never combated by common sense.

"Vanity is never foreign to these false ideas, which are always of a nature to flatter one's *amour propre.*

"We love to rejoice beforehand in the triumph that we believe will win and, aided by mental frivolity, we do not wish to admit that success can be doubted.

"The dislike of making an effort, however, would quickly conceal, with its languishing voice, the wise words of common sense, if we would listen momentarily to them.

"And, lastly, it is necessary to consider credulity, to which, in our opinion, is accorded a place infinitely more honorable than it deserves."

And now the sage, Yoritomo, establishes the argument that, by the aid of common sense, characterized these opinions.

According to him, "It does not belong to new and vibrating souls, as many would have us believe.

"When credulity does not proceed from inveterate stupidity, it is always the result of apathy and weakness.

"Unhappiness and misfortune attend those who are voluntarily feeble.

"Their defect deprived them of the joy derived from happy efforts. They will be the prey of duplicity and untruth.

"They are the vanquished in life, and scarcely deserve the pity of the conqueror; for their defeat lacks grandeur, since it has never been glorified by the majestic strength of conflict."

Following this, the Shogun speaks to us of those whom he calls the ardent seekers after illusion:

"Some sailors started off for an island, which they perceived in the distance.

"It looked like a large, detached red spot, amid the flaming rays of the setting sun, and the sailors told of a thousand wonders about this unknown land, as yet untrodden by human feet.

"The first days of the journey were delightful. The oars lay in the bottom of the boat untouched, and they just allowed themselves to drift with the tide. They disembarked, singing to the murmur of the waters, and gathered the fruits growing on the shores, to appease their hunger.

"But the stream, which was bearing them onward, *did* not retain long its limpidity and repose; the eddies soon entrapped the tiny bark and dragged the sailors overboard.

"Some, looking backward, were frightened at the thought of ascending the river, which had become so tempestuous.

"Escaping the wreckage of the boat as best they could, they entrusted themselves again to the fury of the waters.

"They had to suffer from cold and hunger, for they were far from shore, and as, in their imagination, the island was very near, they had neglected to furnish themselves with the necessities of life.

"At last, after the fatigues which forethought would have prevented, they found themselves one evening, at sundown, at the base of a great rock, bathed in the rosy light of the departing sun.

"This, then, was the island of their dreams.

"Tired out and exhausted from lack of food, they had only the strength to lie down upon the inhospitable rock, there to die!

"The disappearance of the illusion, having destroyed their courage and having struck them with the sword of despair, the rock of reality had proved destructive of their bodies and souls.

"The moral of this story easily unfolds itself.

"If the seekers after illusions had admitted common sense to their deliberations, they would certainly have learned to know the nature of the enchanted isle, and they would have taken good care not to start out on their journey, which must terminate by such a deception.

"Would they not have taken the necessary precaution to prevent all the delays attendant upon travels of adventure, and would they have entrusted their lives to so frail a skiff, if they had acquired common sense?"

We must conclude, with Yoritomo, that illusion could often be transformed into happy reality if it were better understood, and if, instead of looking upon it through the dreams of our imagination, we applied ourselves to the task of eliminating the fluid vapors which envelop it, that we might clothe it anew with the garment of common sense.

Many enterprises have been considered as illusions because we have neglected to awaken the possibilities that lay dormant within them.

The initial thought, extravagant as it may appear, brings with it, at times, facilities of realization that a judgment dictated by common sense can alone make us appreciate.

Only those who know how to keep a strict watch over themselves will be able to escape the causes of disillusion, which lead us through fatal paths of error, to the brink of despair.

"That which is above all to be shunned," said the philosopher, "is the encroachment of discouragement, the result of repeated failures.

"Rare are those who wish to admit their mistakes.

"In the structure of the mind, inaccuracy brings a partial deviation from the truth, and it does not take long for this slight error to generalize itself, if not corrected by its natural reformer—common sense.

"But how many, among those who suffer from these unhappy illusions, are apt to recognize them as such?

"It would, however, be a precious thing for us to admit the causes that have led us to such a sorry result, by never permitting them to occur again.

"This would be the only way for the victims of illusion to preserve the life of that element of success and happiness known as hope.

"Because of seeing so often the good destroyed, we wish to believe no more in it as inherent in our being, and rather than suffer repeatedly from its disappearance, we prefer to smother it before perfect development.

"The greater number of skeptics are only the unavowed lovers of illusion; their desires, never being those capable of realization, they have lost the habit of hoping for a favorable termination of any sentiment.

"The lack of common sense does not allow them to understand the folly of their enterprise, and rather than seek the causes of their habitual failures, they prefer to attack God and humankind, both of whom they hold responsible for all their unhappiness.

"They are willingly ironical, easily become pessimists, and vilify life, without desiring to perceive that it reserved as many smiles for them as the happy people whom they envy.

"All these causes of disappointment can only be attributed to the lack of equilibrium of the reasoning power and, above all, to the absence of common sense, hence we can not judge of relative values.

"To give a definite course to the plans which we form is to prepare the happy termination of them.

"This is also the way to banish seductive illusion, the devourer of beautiful ambitions and youthful aspirations."

And, with his habitual sense of the practical in life, Yoritomo adds the following:

"There are, however, some imaginations which can not be controlled by the power of reasoning, and which, in spite of everything, escape toward the unlimited horizons of the dream.

"It would be in vain to think of shutting them up in the narrow prison walls of strict reason; they would die wishing to attempt an escape.

"To these we can prescribe the dream under its most august form, that of science.

"Each inventor has pursued an illusion, but those whose names have lived to reach our recognition, have caught a glimpse of the vertiginous course they were following, and no longer have allowed themselves to get too far away from their base—science.

"Yes, illusion can be beautiful, on condition that it is not constantly debilitated.

"To make it beautiful we must be its master, then we may attempt its conquest.

"It is thus that all great people act; before adopting an illusion, as truth, they have assured themselves of the means by the aid of which they were permitted first to hope for its transformation and afterward be certain of their power to discipline it.

"Illusion then changes its name and becomes the Ideal.

"Instead of remaining an inaccessible myth, it is transformed into an entity for the creation of good.

"It is no longer the effort to conquer the impossible, which endeavor saps our vital forces; it is a contingency that study and common sense strip of all fortuitous principles, in order to give a form that becomes more tangible and more definite every day.

"We have nothing more to do with sterile efforts toward gaining an object which fades from view and disappears as one approaches it.

"It is no longer the painful reaching out after an object always growing more indistinct as we draw near it.

"It is through conscious and unremitting effort that we attain the happy expression of successful endeavor and realize the best in life, for slow ascension in winning the *best* leaves no room for satiety in this noble strife.

"We must pity those who live for an illusion as well as those whose imagination has not known how to create an ideal, whose beauty illumines their efforts.

"It is the triumph of common sense to accomplish this transformation and to banish empty reveries, replacing them by creating a desire for the *best*, which each one can satisfy—without destroying it.

"The day when this purpose is accomplished, illusion, definitely conquered, will cease to haunt the mind of those whom common sense has illumined; vagaries will make place for reason and terrible disillusion will follow its chief (whose qualities never rise above mediocrity) into his retreat, and allow the flower of hope to blossom in the souls already filled with peace—that quality which is born of reason and common sense."

Lesson III

The Development of the Reasoning Power

When reading certain passages in the manuscripts of Yoritomo, one is forcibly reminded of the familiar phrase: "Nothing is definitely finished among humankind, for each thing stops only to begin again."

He says, "That many centuries before the great minds constructed altars to the goddess of Reason, they were in search of a divinity to replace the one they had just destroyed.

"If it were proposed to me to build temples which would synthesize my devotion with certain sentiments, my desire would be that those dedicated to the *Will* and to *Reason* should dominate all others, for then they would be under the protection of powers for *good*."

In a few pages further on he insists again and again upon the necessity of developing the worship of reason.

"Reasoning," he continues, "is a divinity, around which gravitate a whole world of gods, important but inferior to it.

"Among this people of these idols, so justly revered, there is one god, which occupies a place apart from the others.

"This god is Common Sense, which gave birth to Reason, and has always been its faithful companion.

"It is, in reality, the controlling force exercising its power to guard reason against the predominating character and nefarious tendencies created by self-interest.

"Common sense compels reason to admit principles whose justice it has already recognized, and, at the same time, incites reason to reject those whose absurdity it has demonstrated.

"Common sense allies itself with reason, in order to make that selection of ideas which personal interest can either set aside entirely or modify by illogical inference.

"Reason obeys certain laws, all of which can be united in one sentiment—common sense."

This statement could be illustrated symbolically by comparing its truth to a fan, whose blades converge toward a central point where they remain fixed.

Applying the precept to the picture, the old Shogun gives the design, which we are faithfully copying.

"In this ideal fan," explains Yoritomo, "not only the true reproduction of the qualities directing the progress of knowledge must be perceived, but the symbol of their development must be traced.

"All of these qualities are born of common sense, to which they are closely allied, unfolding and disclosing a luminous radiance.

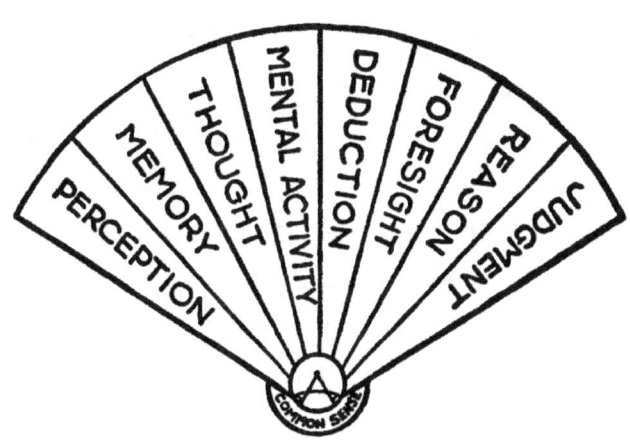

"Although each one may have its autonomy, they never separate, and, even as a fan from which one blade has disappeared can only remain an imperfect object little to be desired, even so, the symbolic fan of reasoning, when it does not unite all the required qualities, becomes a mutilated power, which can only betray the destiny originally attributed to it.

"Consequently, starting from common sense as the central point of reasoning, we find, first, perception.

"This is the action by which exterior things are brought near to us.

"Perception is essentially visual and auditory, although it influences all our senses.

"For example, the fact of tasting a fruit is a perception.

"The seeing of a landscape is equally one.

"The hearing of a song is also a perception.

"In a word, everything which presents itself to us, coming in contact with one of our senses, is a perception; otherwise, the inception of an idea.

"This is the first degree of reasoning.

"Immediately following is memory, without which nothing could be proved.

"It is memory, which, by renewing the motive power of reason, allows us to judge of the proportion of things, grasped by the senses in the present as related to those, which come to us from the past.

"Without memory it would be impossible to make a mental comparison.

"It would be most difficult to determine the true nature of an event, announced by perception, if an analogous sensation, previously experienced, had not just permitted us to classify it by close examination or by differentiating it.

"Memory is a partial resurrection of a past life, whose reconstruction has just permitted us to attribute a true value to the phases of existence.

"It is in preserving the memory of things that we are called upon to compare them and then to judge of them.

"Thought is produced immediately after perception, and the recollection, very often automatic, that it creates within us.

"It is the inception of the idea, which it engenders by a series of results.

"Thought permits the mind to exercise its judgment without allowing it to be influenced by the greatness or humility of the idea.

"By virtue of corresponding recollections, it will associate the present perception with the past representations, and will take an extension, more or less pronounced, according to the degree of intellectuality of the thinker, and according to the importance of the object of its reflections.

"But rarely does the idea present itself alone.

"One thought almost always produces the manifestation of similar thoughts, which group themselves around the first idea as birds of the same species direct their flight toward the same country.

"Thought is the manifestation of the intellectual life; it palpitates in the human brain as does the heart in the breast.

"It is thought which distinguishes humans from animals, who have only instinct to guide them.

"It can be admitted, however, that this instinct is a kind of obscure thought for these inferior beings, from which reflection is eliminated, or, at least, reveals itself only as a vassal of material appetite.

"But with creatures who have intelligence, thought is a superior faculty, which aids the soul to free itself from the bondage of vulgar and limited impressions.

"When perception, memory, and thought unite to form judgment, activity of mind will become necessary, in order to accelerate the production of ideas in extending the field of imagination.

"Moral inertia is the most deplorable of all defects; it retards intellectual growth and hinders the development of personality.

"It is, in this understanding, the enemy of common sense, for it will admit voluntarily a reasoning power, existing *per se*, rather than make the necessary effort which will set free the truth and constitute an individual opinion.

"Vulgarity is, then, almost always the sign of mental sloth.

"It is not infrequent to see a mind of real capacity fall into error, where an intelligence of mediocre caliber asserts its efficiency. Indifference is the most serious obstacle to the attainment of judgment.

"Common sense demands a keen alertness of understanding, placed at the disposal of a reflection which appears at times slow of action, but which is long in being manifested only because of the desire to surround itself by all the guaranties of truth concerning the object in question.

"The fifth blade of the fan is the quality of deduction the most solid basis for the judgments which are formed by common sense.

"By deduction we are able to solve all relative questions with perfect accuracy.

"It is by abstracting reckless contingencies, and by relying only upon the relativeness of facts, that we can succeed in discovering the truth that there are too many representations as to these facts.

"Deduction is the great support of mental weakness. It helps in discerning proportions, possibilities, even as it helps in skillfully avoiding the fear of error."

This will be discussed in detail in Lesson Seven of this book.

"Foresight," he continues, "is rightly looked upon as one of the indispensable elements in cultivating common sense.

"The faculty of foresight always accompanies common sense, in order to strengthen its qualities of skill and observation.

"One must not confound, as many people are tempted to do, foresight and conjecture.

"The first consists in taking great care to prevent the repetition of unhappy facts, which have already existed.

"Foresight will exert an influence on future events by establishing an analogy between them and the actual incidents that, of necessity, will lead to the adoption or rejection of present projects.

"It is to be observed that all these faculties are subordinate, one to the other, and, in proportion to the unfolding of the fan, we can prove that all the blades previously mentioned have concurred in the formation of the blade of which we are now speaking.

"In order to foresee disasters it is necessary that the perception—visual or auditory—of said disasters should already have impressed us. We have kept intact the memory of them, since it is reconstructed emotion that guides our thoughts.

"These same thoughts, in extending themselves, form groups of thoughts harmonious in character, all relative to the one, which is the object of the debate.

"Our minds become more active in recalling the incidents, the remembrance of which marks the time that has elapsed between the old perception and the present state of mental absorption.

"The faculty of deduction, which is born of these different mental conflicts, permits me to foresee that circumstances of the same nature will lead to others similar to those we have already mentioned.

"We have merely sketched rapidly the scale of sensations which follow each other, in order to reach the explanation of how foresight is formed.

"By assimilating these present facts with those of the past, we are permitted to draw a conclusion, relating to the same group of results, because of the conformity of those past facts to the present questions.

"Foresight is passive; between it and precaution there is the same difference as between theory and practice.

"Precaution is preeminently active, and it marks its first appearance by means of foresight, but does not stop in this effort until it has rendered foresight productive.

"It is well to foresee, but it is precious to preclude.

"The second part of the act of precaution can, however, only be accomplished after having permitted the brain to register the thoughts which determine the first part of this act."

In order to understand this very subtle difference, but very important one, which classifies these two sentiments, the old sage gives us the following example:

"Let us suppose," he says, "that, on a beautiful day in spring, a man starts out for an excursion which will last until the dawn of the following day.

"If he has common sense, he will say to himself that the sun will not be shining at the time of his return, that the nights of spring are cold, and that this one will be no exception to the rule.

"This is foresight.

"If common sense, with all its consequences, takes possession of him, it will increase his power of reasoning. He will think that, in order to avoid suffering from the change of temperature, it would be well to cover himself with a cloak.

"And, even though the sun shone, he would not hesitate to furnish himself with this accessory, which in fact will render him the greatest service.

"This is precaution.

"This quality is indispensable to the formation of the reasoning power; for, in addition to the necessity of foreseeing certain results, it permits also of directing their course, if it be impossible to exempt them completely.

"Reasoning is the art of developing, to the highest degree, the suppositions resulting from deduction.

"One is usually mistaken as to the exact meaning of the words 'to reason,' and people seldom attach the importance to them that they should.

"One is apt to think that the gift of reasoning is bestowed upon every one. Perhaps; but to reason, following the principles of justice and truth, is an operation which can only be performed by minds endowed with common sense.

"In order to arrive at this result, it is essential to impress upon oneself the value of the words, 'to deduct accurately,' after having produced the radiation of thoughts which depend upon the object in question, and to foresee the consequences of the facts that a resolution could determine.

"Above all, to avoid contentment with the *approximate*, which conceals many pitfalls under false appearances.

"Without permitting oneself to express useless trivialities, not to neglect to become impregnated with those axioms which have been rightfully baptized, 'wisdom of nations.'

"They are generally based on a secular observation, and are the product of many generations.

"It would be puerile to attach vital importance to them, but one would surely regret having entirely scorned their counsel.

"Too much erudition is at times detrimental to reason, based on common sense. Although fully appreciating science, and devoting serious study to it, we would do well to introduce the human element into our knowledge.

"There are some essential truths which modify daily life without, for this reason, lessening their importance.

"Some of them are of premature development; others are of miniature growth.

"To reason without offending common sense, it is, therefore, indispensable to consider time, place, environment, and all the contingencies which could arise to undermine the importance of reasoning."

After having reviewed all these phases, we shall then extend, in accord with Yoritomo, the last blade of this rudimentary fan, and we shall find judgment.

"This one is the index to that quality of mind called *conviction*.

"This mental operation consists in drawing together many ideas that their relative characteristics may be determined.

"This operation takes the place contiguous to reasoning, of which it is the result.

"Judgment determines its character after having registered the reasons which ought to indicate its position; it deducts the conclusions imposed by the explanatory principle, and classifies the idea by submitting it to the valuation placed upon it by judgment.

"All judgment is either affirmative or negative.

"It can never be vacillating or neutral.

"In this last case it will assume the title of opinion, and will attribute to itself the definite qualities that characterize judgment.

"It is, however, at times subjected to certain conditions, where the principles on which it is based are not sufficiently defined, and, therefore, becomes susceptible to a change, either of form or of nature.

"It is possible, without violating the laws of common sense, to establish a judgment whose terms will be modified by the mutation of causes.

"But common sense demands that these different influences should be foreseen, and that these eventualities should be mentioned when pronouncing the judgment."

We have reached the last blade of the symbolic fan, described by the philosopher, for many secondary qualities may be placed between the principle blades.

But faithful to his explanatory method, he wished to indicate to us the broad lines first, and also to state the indispensable faculties constituting common sense, by teaching us their progression and development.

He desired to demonstrate to us also how much all these qualities would be lessened in value if they were not united and bound together in the order in which they ought to manifest themselves.

"We have all possessed," said he, "some fans whose point of reunion was destroyed in part or altogether lost.

"What becomes of it, then?

"During a certain length of time, always rather short, the blades, after having remained bound together by the thread which holds them, separate, when it is severed because of the lack of harmony and of equilibrium at their base.

"Very soon, one blade among them detaches itself, and the mutilated fan takes its place in the cemetery where sleep those things deteriorated because of old age or disuse.

"It is the same with the qualities which we have just enumerated. As long as they remain attached to their central point, which is common sense, they stand erect, beautiful and strong, concurring in the fertilization of our minds, and in creating peace in our lives.

"But if the point of contact ceases to maintain them, to bind them together, to forbid their separating, we shall soon see them fall apart after having escaped from the temporary protection of the secondary qualities.

"For a while we seek to evoke them; but recognizing the ruse existing in their commands, we shall soon be the first to abandon them, in order to harmonize our favors with the deceptive mirage of the illusions; at least, if we do not allow ourselves to be tempted by fallacious arguments of vanity.

"In the one as in the other case, we shall become, then, the prey of error and ignorance, for common sense is the intelligence of truth."

Lesson IV

Common Sense and Impulse

Impulsive people are those who allow themselves to be guided by their initial impressions and make resolutions or commit acts under the domination of a special consciousness into which perception has plunged them.

Impulse is a form of cerebral activity that forces us to make a movement before the mind is able to decide upon it by means of reflection or reasoning. The Shogun deals with it at length and defines it thus:

"Impulse is an almost direct contact between perception and result.

"Memory, thought, deduction, and, above all, reason are absolutely excluded from these acts, which are never inspired by intellectuality.

"The impression received by the brain is immediately transmuted into an act, similar to those acts which depend entirely on automatic memory.

"It is certain in making a series of movements, which compose the act of walking upstairs or the action of walking from one place to another, we do not think of analyzing our efforts and this act of walking almost limits itself to an organic function, so little does thought enter into its composition.

"In the case of repeated impulses, it can be absolutely affirmed that substance is the antecedent and postulate of the essence of being.

"Substance comprises all corporal materiality: instinctive needs, irrational movements—in a word, all actions where common sense is not a factor.

"Essence is that imponderable part of being which includes the soul, the mind, the intelligence, in fact the entire mentality.

"It is this last element of our being which crystallizes our thoughts, classifies them, and leads us to common sense, by means of reasoning and judgment.

"Those who, having received an injury from their superiors, reply to it at once by corresponding affront, are absolutely sure to become the victims of their impulses.

"It is only when the act is consummated, that they will think of the consequences which it can entail; the loss of employment first, then punishment, in severity according to the gravity of the offense; lastly, misery, perhaps the result of forced inactivity.

"On the contrary, those who are endowed with common sense will reflect in a flash, by recalling all the different phases which we have described. Their intelligence, being appealed to, will represent to them the consequences of a violent action.

"They will find, in common sense, the strength not to respond to an injury at once; but will not forego the right, however, of avenging themselves under the guise of a satisfaction which will be all the more easily accorded to them as their moderation will not fail to make an impression in their favor."

"There is, between common sense and impulse," says Yoritomo, "the difference that one would find between two coats, one of which was bought ready-made, while the other, after being cut according to the proportions of the one who is to wear it, was sewed by a tailor to whom all the resources of the art are known."

If impulses adopt the same character for every one, common sense adapts itself to the mind, to the sensitiveness, to the worth of those who practice it; it is a garment which is adjusted to the proportions of its owner, and, according to that person's taste, is elaborate or simple.

Certain people have a tendency to confound intuition and impulse.

These two things, really very different in essence, are only related by spontaneity of thought that gives them birth.

But whereas intuition, a sensation altogether moral, concisely stated, is composed of mental speculations, impulses always resolve themselves into acts and resolutions to act.

Intuition is a sort of obscure revelation, which reason controls only after its formation.

Impulse never engages common sense in the achievements, which it realizes. It never decides upon them in advance, and almost always engenders regrets.

It is the result of a defeat in self-control, which will power and the power of reasoning alone can correct.

Intuition is less spontaneous than impulse.

It is a very brief mental operation, but, nevertheless, very real, which, very indistinctly, touches lightly all the phases of reasoning, in order to reach a conclusion so rapidly that those who conceive it have difficulty in making transformations of the initial thought intelligible.

It is nonetheless true that intuition is always inspired by a predicted reflection, but in spite of this fact, an existing reflection.

Impulse, on the contrary, only admits instinct as its source of existence.

It is the avowed enemy of common sense, which counsels the escape from exterior insinuations that one may concentrate, in order to listen to the voice which dictates to us the abstinence from doing anything until after making a complete analysis of the cause which agitates us.

Some philosophers have sought to rank inspiration under the flag of impulse, which they thought to defend; yes, even to recover esteem under this new form.

"We should know how to stand on guard," says Yoritomo, "against this fatal error."

"Inspiration," says he "is rarely immobilized under the traits which characterized its first appearance.

"Before expressing itself in a work of art or of utility, it was the embryo of that which it must afterward personify.

"The ancients when relating that a certain divinity sprang, fully armed, from the head of a god, accredited this belief to instantaneous creation.

"If musicians, painters, poets, and inventors want to be sincere, they will agree that, between the thought which they qualify as inspiration, and its tangible realization, a ladder of transformations has been constructed, and that it is only by progressive steps that they have attained what seemed to them the nearest to perfection."

Impulse, then, is only distantly related to inspiration and intuition.

Let us add that these gifts are very often only the fruit of an unconscious mental effort, and that, most of the time, the thoughts, which in good faith one accepts as inspiration or intuition, are only nameless reminiscences, whose apparition coincides with an emotional state of being, which existed at the time of the first perception.

There, again, the presence of reasoning is visible, and also the presence of common sense, which tries to convert into a work of lasting results those impressions which would probably remain unproductive without the aid of these two faculties.

Impulses are, most of the time, the vassals of material sensations.

Definite reasoning and impartial judgment, inspired by common sense, are rarely the possession of a sick person.

Sufferings, in exposing people to melancholy, make them see things in a defective light; the effort of thinking fatigues a weak brain, and the fear of a resolution that would force them to get out of inactivity has enormous influence upon the deductions that dictate their judgment.

Before discussing the advantages of conflict, they will instinctively be resigned to inertia.

If, on the contrary, their temperament disposes them to anger, they will compromise an undertaking by a spontaneous violence, which patience and reflection would otherwise have made successful. It is possible also that a valiant soul is unable to obey a weak body, and that instinct, awakened by fear, leads one on to the impulsive desires of activity.

Inadequate food or excessive nourishment can produce impulses of a different nature, but these differences are wholly and completely distinct as to character.

The most evident danger of impulses lies in the scattering of mental forces, which, being too frequently called upon, use themselves up without benefiting either reason or common sense.

The habit of indulging in movements dictated only by instinct, in suppressing all the phases of judgment leaves infinitely more latitude to caprice, which exists at the expense of solid judgment.

Perception, being related to that which interests our passions, by getting in direct contact with the action which should simply be derived from a deduction, inspired by common sense, multiplies the unreflected manifestations and produces waste of the forces, which should be concentrated on a central point, after having passed through all the phases of which we have spoken.

In addition, the permanency of resolutions is unknown to impulsive people.

Their tendency, by leading them on toward instantaneous solutions, allows them to ignore the benefits of consistency.

"They are like unto a peasant," said the old Nippon, "who owned a field in the country of Tokyo. Scarcely had he begun to sow a part of the field when, under the influence of an unhappy impulse, he plowed up the earth again in order to sow the ground with a new seed.

"If he heard any one speak of any special new method of cultivation, he only tried it for a short while, and then abandoned it, to try another way.

"He tried to cultivate rice; then, before the time for harvesting it, he became enthusiastic for the cultivation of chrysanthemums, which he abandoned very soon in order to plant trees, whose slow development incited him to change his nursery into a field of wheat.

"He died in misery, a victim of his having scorned the power of consistency and common sense."

Now Yoritomo, after having put us on our guard against impulses, shows us the way to conquer these causes of disorder.

"To control unguarded movements, which place us on a level with inferior beings. That is," said he "in making us dependent on one instinct alone. This is," said he, "to take the first step toward the *will* to think, which is one of the forms of common sense.

"In order to reach this point, the first resolution to make is to escape from the tyranny of the body, which tends to replace the intellectual element in impulsive people.

"When I was still under the instruction of my preceptor, Lang-Ho, I saw him cure a man who was affected with what he called 'The Malady of the First Impulse.'

"Whether it concerned good actions or reprehensible ones, this man always acted without the least reflection.

"To launch a new enterprise, which the most elementary common sense condemned, he gave the greater part of his fortune in a moment of enthusiasm.

"He allowed himself to commit acts of violence that taught him severe lessons.

"Finally, vexed beyond measure, dissatisfied with himself and others, he so brutally maltreated a high dignitary in a moment of violent anger that the latter sent for him that he might punish him. Learning of this, the man, crazy with rage, rushed out of his house in order to kill the prince with his own hand.

"It was in this paroxysm of passion that my master met him. Like all impulsive people, he was full of his subject, and, joining the perception of the insult to the judgment of it, which his instinct had immediately dictated to him, he did not conceal his murderous intentions.

"My master, by means of a strategy, succeeded in dissuading him from accomplishing his revenge that day. He persuaded him that the prince was absent and would only return to town upon the following day.

"The man believed him, and allowed himself to be taken to the house of Lang-Ho.

"But it was in vain that Lang-Ho unfolded all his most subtle arguments. Neither the fear of punishment, nor the hope of pardon, could conquer the obstinacy, which can always be observed in impulsive people when their resolution has not accomplished its purpose.

"It was then that my master employed a ruse, whose fantastic character brings a smile, but which, however, demonstrates a profound knowledge of the human heart when acting under the influence of common sense.

"During the sleep of his guest, Lang-Ho took away his robe, replacing it by a garment made of two materials. One was golden yellow, the other a brilliant green. After attacks of terrible anger, in spite of the solicitation of his impulsive nature, which incited him to go out, he did not dare to venture into the streets in such a costume.

"That which the most subtle arguments had been unable to accomplish, was obtained through fear of ridicule.

"Two days passed; his fury was changed into great mental exhaustion, because impulsive people cannot withstand the contact with obstacles for any length of time.

"It was this moment which my master chose to undertake the cure, in which he was so vitally interested.

"With the most delicate art, he explained to the impulsive man all the chain of sentiments leading from perception to judgment.

"He caused common sense to intervene so happily that the man was permeated by it. My master kept him near by for several weeks, always using very simple arguments to combat the instinctive resolutions, which were formulated in his brain many times a day.

"Common sense, thus solicited, was revealed to the impulsive one, and appeared like a peaceful counselor.

"The ridiculous and odious side of his resolution was represented to him with such truth that he embraced Lang-Ho, saying:

"'Now, Master, I can go away, and your mind can be at rest about me.

"'The arguments of common sense have liberated me from bondage in which my lack of reflection held me.

"'I return to my home, but I beg of you, allow me to take away this ridiculous costume that was my savior.

"'I wish to hang it in my home, in the most conspicuous place, that, from the moment my nature incites me to obey the commands of impulse, I may be able to look at once upon this garment, and thus recall your teachings, which have brought sweetness and peace into my life.'"

All those who are inclined to act by instinct should follow this example, not by dressing up in a ridiculous robe half green and half yellow, but by placing obstacles in the way of the accomplishment of impulsive acts, which the dictates of common sense would not sanction.

"For those whose mind possess a certain delicacy," again says the old master, "these obstacles will be of a purely moral order, but for those who voluntarily allow themselves to be dominated by a diseased desire for action, obstacles should adopt a tangible form; the difficulty in conquering anything always makes impulsive people reflect a little.

"Under the immediate impression of the perception of an act they are ready for a struggle to the death; but this ardor is quickly extinguished, and inertia, in its turn, having become an impulse, makes them throw far away from them the object which determined the effort.

"In proportion as they encounter obstacles, which they have taken the precaution to raise, the encroachment of the impression will make itself less felt.

"The mere fact of having foreseen will become a matter for reflection for them.

"The feeling of the responsibilities will be roused in them, and they will understand how difficult it is to escape the consequences of impulsive acts."

Would one not say that these lines had been written yesterday?

More than ever our age of unrest makes us the prey of impulses, and to the majority of our contemporaries, the robe, half green and half yellow (by recalling to them the worship of common sense), will become a fetish, more precious than all the amulets with which superstition loves to adorn logic, or to incorporate fantastic outline in the classic setting of beautiful jewels.

Lesson V
The Dangers of Sentimentality

The Shogun says: "There are sentimentalities of many kinds, some present less dangers than others, but from every point of view they are prejudicial to the acquisition and exercise of common sense. To cultivate sentiment over which the Will has no control is always to be regretted. Sentimentality is multiform.

"It presents itself, at times, under the aspect of an obscure appeal to sensuality and brings with it a passing desire of the heart and of the senses, which produces an artificial appreciation of the emotion felt.

"In this first case sentimentality is an unconscious manifestation of egotism, because, outside of that which provokes this outward manifestation, everything is alienated and becomes indistinct.

"The incidents of existence lose their true proportion, since everything becomes relative to the object because of our preoccupation.

"The impulse reigns supreme there when sentimentality establishes itself, and the desire of judgment, if it makes itself apparent, is quickly shunned, to the profit of illusory reasons, in which pure reason does not intervene.

"This sentimentality amalgamating the springs of egotism bereaves the soul's longing of all its greatness.

"The anxiety to attribute all our impressions to *emotion is* only a way of intensifying it for our personal satisfaction, at the expense of a sentiment far deeper and more serious, which never blossoms under the shadow of egotism and of frivolous sentimentality.

"Never will common sense have the chance to manifest itself in those who permit such ephemeral and enfeebling impressions to implant themselves in their souls.

"However they must be pitied because their artificial emotion often results in a sorrow which is not lessened by repetition, but whose manifestation is none the less prejudicial to the peace of their being.

"All those who do not harmonize common sense and the emotions of the heart become passive to the investiture of a sentimentality which does not wait to know if the object be worthy of them before it exists in consciousness.

"From this state of mind arise disillusions and their recurrence entails a defect in the conception.

"People who are often deceived in allowing themselves to feel a sorrow which is only based on the longings of sentimentality become pessimists quickly and deny the existence of deep and enduring affection judged from its superior expression.

"This superior expression of sentiment is freed from all personality and such judgment, which differentiates it from other sentiments.

"If we wished to appeal to common sense we should acknowledge, too often, that in the search for expansion we have only recognized the opportunity to satisfy the inclination which urges us to seek for pleasure.

"Sentiment reasons, and is capable of devotion. Sentimentality excludes reflective thought and ignores generosity.

"We are capable of sacrificing ourselves for sentiment.

"Sentimentality exacts the sacrifice of others.

"Therefore, profiting by the principles already developed, those who cultivate common sense will never fail to reason in the following manner:

"Opening the symbolic fan, they will encounter, after perfection, the memory which will suggest the recollections of personal and strange experiences and they will record this fact: abnegation is rarely encountered.

"The inclination of our thoughts will suggest to us the difficulties there are in searching for it.

"Deduction will acquaint us with the temerity of this exaction, and precaution will attract our thoughts to the possibility of suffering which could proceed from disillusion.

"Following this, reasoning and judgment will intervene in order to hasten the conclusion formulated by common sense.

"It follows then that, abnegation being so rare, common sense indicates to me that it would be imprudent for me to allow my happiness to rest upon the existence of a thing so exceptional.

"For this reason this sentimental defect will find common sense armed against this eventuality.

"There is another form of sentimentality not less common.

"It is that which extends itself to all the circumstances of life and transforms true pity into a false sensibility, the exaggeration of which deteriorates the true value of things.

"Those who give publicity to this form of sentiment are agitated (or imagine themselves to be agitated) as profoundly on the most futile of pretexts as for the most important cause.

"They do not think to ask themselves if their ardor is merited; also every such experience, taking out of them something of their inner selves, leaves them enfeebled and stranded.

"Every excursion into the domain of sentimentality is particularly dangerous, for tourists always fail to carry with them the necessary coinage which one calls common sense."

After having put ourselves on guard against the surprises of mental exaggeration, Yoritomo warns us of a kind of high respectable sentimentality that we possess, that is nonetheless censurable because under an exterior of the purest tenderness it conceals a profound egotism.

It concerns paternal love from which reasoning and common sense are excluded.

"Nothing" said he "seems more noble than the love of parents for their children, and no sentiment is more august when it is comprehended in all its grandeur.

"But how many people are apt to distinguish it from an egotistical sentimentality.

"I have seen some mothers oppose the departure of their sons, preferring to oblige them to lead an obscure existence near to them, rather than impose upon themselves the sorrow of a separation.

"These women do not fail to condemn the action of others, who, filled with a sublime abnegation, allow their children to depart, hiding from them the tears which they shed, because they have the conviction of seeing them depart for the fortune and the happiness which they feel themselves unable to offer them.

"Which of these are worthy of admiration? Those who condemn their children to a life of mediocrity in order to obey an egotistical sentimentality, or those who, with despair in their hearts, renounce the joy of their presence, and think only of their own grief in order to build upon it the happiness of their dear ones.

"The common sense of this latter class inspiring in them this magnificent sentiment, and forcing them to set aside a sentimentality which is, in reality, only the caricature of sentiment, has permitted them to escape that special kind of egotism, which could be defined thus: The translation of a desire for personal contentment.

"Ought we then to blame others so strongly?

"It is necessary, above all, to teach them to reason about the ardor of their emotions, and only to follow them when they find that they are cleansed from all aspiration which is not a pledge of devotion."

Now the Shogun speaks to us with that subtlety of analysis that is characteristic and refers to a kind of sentimentality the most frequent and the least excusable.

"There are," he tells us, "a number of people who, without knowing that they offend common sense in a most indefensible manner, invoke sentimentality in order to dispense with exercising the most vulgar pity, to the profit of their neighbor.

"A prince," he continues, "possessed a large tract of land which he had put under grain.

"For the harvest, a large number of peasants and laborers were employed and each one lived on the products of his labor.

"But a prolonged drought threatened the crop; so the prince's overseer dismissed most of the laborers, who failed to find employment in the parched country.

"Soon hunger threatened the inmates of the miserable dwellings, and sickness, its inseparable companion, did not fail to follow.

"Facing the conditions the prince left, and had it not been for two or three wealthy and charitable people the laborers would have starved to death.

"This pitiful condition was soon changed, abundance replaced famine, and the master returned to live in his domain.

"But amazement followed when he addressed his people as follows: 'Here I am, back among you, and I hope to remain here a long time; if I left you, it was because I have so great an affection for all my servants and because even the bare thought of seeing them suffer caused me unbearable sorrow.

"I am not among those who are sufficiently hard-hearted to be able to take care of sick and suffering people and to be a witness of their martyrdom. My pity is too keen to permit of my beholding this spectacle; this is why I had to leave to others, less sensitive, the burden of care which my too tender heart was unable to lavish on you."

And that which is more terrible is that this man believed what he said.

He did not understand the monstrous tear, which he made in the robe of common sense, by declaring that he had committed the vilest act of cruelty due to excessive sensitiveness since it represented a murderous act of omission."

Examples of this form of sentimentality are more numerous than we think.

There exist people who cover their dogs with caresses, gorging them with dainties, and will take good care not to succor the needy.

Others faint away at sight of an accident and never think of giving aid to the wounded.

One may observe that for people exercising sentimentality at the expense of common sense, the greatest catastrophe in intensity, if it be far away from us, diminishes, while the merest incident, a little out of the ordinary, affects them in a most immoderate manner if it be produced in the circle of their acquaintances.

It is needless to add that, if it touches them directly, it becomes an unparalleled calamity; it seems that the rest of the world must be troubled by it.

This propensity toward pitying oneself unreasonably about little things which relate to one directly and this exaggerated development of a sterile sentimentality are almost always artificial, and the instinct of self-preservation very often aids in their extermination.

"Among my old disciples," pursues the Shogun, "I had a friend whose son was afflicted by this kind of sentimentality, the sight of blood made him faint and he was incapable of aiding any one whomsoever; that which he called his good heart, and which was only a form of egotistical sentimentality, prevented him from looking at the suffering of others.

"One day, a terrible earthquake destroyed his palace; he escaped, making his way through the ruins and roughly pushing aside the wounded who told about it afterward.

"I saw him some days after; instead of reproaching him severely for his conduct, I endeavored to make him see how false was his conception of pity, since, not only had he not fainted at the sight of those who, half-dead, were groaning, but he had found in the egotistical sentiment of self-preservation the strength to struggle against those who clung to him, beseeching him for help.

"I demonstrated to him the evident contradiction of his instinctive cruelty to the sentimentality that it pleased him to make public.

"I made an appeal to common sense, in order to prove to him the attitude, which he had, until then, assumed, and I had the joy of seeing myself understood.

"My arguments appealed to his mentality, and always afterward, when he had the opportunity to bring puerile sentimentality and common sense face to face, he forced himself to appeal to that quality, which in revealing to him the artifice of the sentiment which animated him, cured him of false sensibility, which he had displayed up to that time."

Sentimentality is in reality only a conception of egotism, under the different forms that it adopts.

Yoritomo proves it to us again, in speaking of the weakness of certain teachers, who, under the pretext of avoiding trouble, allow their children to follow their defective inclinations.

"It is by an instinctive hatred of effort that parents forbid themselves to make their children cry when reprimanding them," said he.

"If the parents wish to be sincere to themselves, they will perceive that the sorrow in seeing their children's tears flow plays a very small part in their preconceived idea of indulgence.

"It is in order to economize their own nervous energy or to avoid cleverly the trouble of continued teaching, that they hesitate to provoke these imaginary miseries, the manifestation of which is caused by the great weakness of the teachers.

"Common sense, nevertheless, ought to make them understand that it is preferable to allow the little ones to shed a few tears, which are quickly dried, rather than to tolerate a deplorable propensity for these habits which, later in life, will cause them real anxiety.

"A very little reasoning could suffice to convince one of the dangers of sentimentality, if the persons who devote themselves entirely to it consented to reflect, by frankly agreeing to the true cause that produces it.

"They would discover in this false pity the desire not to disturb their own tranquility.

"They would also perceive that, in order to spare themselves a few unpleasant moments in the present they are preparing for themselves great sorrow for the future.

"In parental affection, as in friendship or in the emotions of love, sentimentality is none other than an exaggerated amplification of the ego.

"If it be true that all our acts, even those most worthy of approbation, can react in our personality, at least it is necessary that we should be logical and that, in order to create for ourselves a partial happiness or to avoid a temporary annoyance, we should not prepare for ourselves an existence, outlined by deception and fruitless regrets.

"Sentimentality and its derivatives, puerile pity and false sensitiveness, can create illusion for those who do not practice the art of reasoning, but the friends of common sense do not hesitate to condemn them for it.

"In spite of the glitter in which it parades itself, sentimentality will never be anything but the dross of true sentiment."

Lesson VI
The Utility of Common Sense In Daily Life

As our philosopher explains, the influence of common sense is above all appreciation of daily events. "We have," he continues, "very rarely in life the opportunity of making grave decisions, but we are called upon daily to resolve unimportant problems, and we can only do it in a judicious way, if we are allowed to devote ourselves to certain kinds of investigation.

"This is what may be called to judge with discrimination, otherwise, with common sense.

"Without this faculty, it is in vain that our memory amasses the materials, which must serve us in the comparative examination of facts.

"And this examination can only be spoiled by decrepitude, if common sense did not succeed in dictating its conclusions to us.

"Thanks to this faculty, we possess this accuracy of mind which permits us to discern truth from falsehood.

"It is this power that aids us in distinguishing what we should consider as a duty, as a right, or as a thing conforming to equity, established by the laws of intelligence.

"Without common sense we should be like an inexperienced gardener, who, for want of knowledge, would allow the weeds to grow and would neglect the plants whose function is to nourish us.

"In order to conform to the habit of judging with common sense, one ought first to lay down the following principle:

"No fact can exist, unless there is a sufficient motive to determine its nature.

"It is when operating on the elements furnished us by common sense that we are able to discern the quality of the object of our attention.

"One day, a sage, whom people gladly consulted, was asked by what means he had learned to know so well the exact proportion of things, so that he never failed to attribute to them their real value.

"'Why' they added, 'can you foresee so exactly the evil and direct us to that which is right and just?'

"And the superstitious people added:

"'Are you not in communication with the spirits, which float in space, which come from the other world?

"Would you not be counseled by voices which we have not the power to hear, and do you not see things which are visible to you alone?'

"'You are right,' replied the saintly man, smiling:

"'I have indeed the power to hear and to see that which you do not perceive; but sorcery has no relation to the power which is attributed to me.

"If you wish, you will be able to possess it in your turn, for my means are not a secret.

"'I keep my eyes and ears open.'

"And as every one burst out laughing, believing it a joke, the sage began again:

"'But this is not all; after having seen and heard, I call to my aid all the qualities which constitute common sense and, thanks to this faculty, I draw my conclusions from my experience, from which enthusiasm, fancy, as well as personal interest are totally excluded.

"'This done, and my judgment being formulated in my thought, I adapt it to the circumstances, and especially to the material situation and to the mentality of those who consult me.'

"From these counsels," thinks the Shogun, "we must draw a precious lesson.

"It is true that an exigency, physical or moral, can determine, in different individuals, a very different resolution.

"According to the manner of life adopted, or the direction given to one's duties, different resolutions can be made without lacking common sense. It is indisputable that what represents social obligations does not demand the same conduct from the peasant as from the prince.

"We should outrage common sense in presenting a workman with a gorgeous robe suitable for great ceremonies, in which to do his work, but reason would be equally outraged if one put on a shabby costume to go to the palace of the Mikado."

The nature of resolutions inspired by common sense varies according to environment, the time, and the state of mind in which one is.

These conditions make of this quality a virtue really worth acquiring, for it is more difficult to conquer than many others and its effects are of infinite variety.

But as always, Yoritomo, after having signaled the danger, and indicated the remedy, gives us the manner of its application.

That which follows is marked by that simplicity of conception and facility of execution that render the doctrine of the Nippon philosopher absolutely efficacious.

Instead of losing himself by digressing from his subject and by placing himself on the summits of psychology, he remains with us, puts himself on the level of the most humble among us, and says to us all:

"The best way to use common sense in daily life consists in declaring one's honest intentions.

"What should I do if I were in the place of the person with whom I am discussing?

"I found myself one day on the slope of a hill named Yung-Tshi, and I remarked that the majority of the trees were stripped of their foliage.

"The season seeming to me not sufficiently advanced for this condition of vegetation, I expressed my astonishment to a passer-by, who replied to me:

"'Alas! This occurs every year at the same time, and it is not well to cultivate trees on the height of Yung-Tshi, for the sun, being too hot, dries them up before the time when the foliage ought to fall.'

"A few days afterward my steps lead me on the opposite slope of the same hill.

"There the trees were covered with foliage, still green but uncommon, and their appearance indicated an unhealthy condition of growth.

"'Alas!' said a man who was working in the hedges to me, 'it is not well to cultivate trees on the height of Yung-Tshi, for the sun never shines there, and they can only acquire the vigor they would possess if they were planted in another country.'

"And, although recognizing the truth of these two opinions, so contradictory, I could not help thinking that they were the reproduction of those which men, deprived of common sense, express every day.

"The same hill produced a vegetation, affected in different ways, by reason of different causes; and the people, instead of taking into consideration how carelessly they had chosen the location of their plantation, preferred to attribute the defect to the site itself, rather than to their lack of precaution.

"Both of them were suffering from a hurtful exaggeration, but each one explained it in a way arbitrarily exclusive.

"He of the north made out that the sun never shone on the summit of Yung-Tshi, and the inhabitant of the south affirmed that the health-giving shade was unknown there."

This is why it is indispensable to the successful resolution of the thousand and one problems of daily life, both those whose sole importance is derived from their multiplicity and those whose seriousness justly demands our attention, to employ the very simple method which prescribes that we place ourselves mentally in the position and circumstances of the person with whom we are discussing.

If each one of the inhabitants of Yung-Tshi had followed this precept, instead of declaring that the hill never received the sun or that shade never fell upon it, they would each one have thought for himself.

"At what conclusions should I arrive, if I had planted my trees on the opposite side?"

From the reasoning, which would have ensued, the following truth would most certainly have been revealed.

"If I were in the other man's place, I should certainly think as he does."

This premise once laid down, the conclusion would be reached; all the more exact, because, without abandoning their arguments, each one would present those, which it is easy to turn against an adversary.

Before solving a problem, those who desire to avoid making a mistake must never fail to ask themselves this question:

What should I do if my interests were those of the opposite party?

Or, yet again:

What should I reply if my adversaries used the same language to me as I purpose using when addressing them?

This method is valuable in that it raises unexpected objections, which the mind would not consider if one had simply studied the question from one's own point of view.

It is a self-evident fact that, according to the state of mind in which we are, things assume different proportions in the rendering of judgment on them.

We must not argue as children do, who, not having the sense of calculating distances, ask how the man standing near to them will be able to enter his house, which they see far away, and which seems to them of microscopic dimensions.

One departs from common sense when one attributes to insignificant things a fundamental value.

We neglect to consider it in a most serious way when we adopt principles contrary to the general consensus of opinion accredited in the environment in which we are living.

"A high dignitary of the court," says Yoritomo, "would be lacking in common sense if he wished to conduct himself as a peasant and, on the other hand, a peasant would give a proof of great folly were he to attempt the remodeling of his life on the principles adopted by courtiers.

"Those who, passing their lives in camps, wish to think and to act like philosophers, whose books are their principal society, would cause people to doubt their wisdom; and the thinkers who should adopt publicly the methods of a swashbucklers would only inspire contempt."

In ordinary life, one ought to consider this faculty of common sense as the ruling principle of conduct.

One can be lacking in thought, in audacity, in brilliant qualities, if only one possesses commonsense.

It takes the place of intelligence in many people, whose minds, unaccustomed to subtle argument, only lend themselves to very simple reasoning.

A versatile mentality rarely belongs to such minds, because it is not their *forte* to unfold hidden truths.

It walks in the light and keeps in the very middle of the road, far from the ambushes that may be concealed by the hedges of the crossroads.

Many people gifted with common sense but deprived of ordinary intelligence have amassed a fortune, but never, no matter how clever they may be, have people known success, if they have not strictly observed the laws of common sense.

It is not only in debates that the presence of this virtue should make itself felt, but every act of our life should be impregnated with it.

There are no circumstances, no matter how insignificant they may appear, where the intervention of common sense would be undesirable.

It is only common sense that will indicate the course of conduct to be pursued, so as not to hurt the feelings or offend the prejudices of other people.

There are great savants, whose science, freed from all puerile beliefs, rises above current superstition.

They would consider it a great lack of common sense if they expounded their theories before the humble minded, whose blind faith would be injured thereby.

Of two things one is certain: either they would refuse to believe such theories and this display of learning would be fruitless, or their habitual credulity would be troubled and they would lose their tranquility without acquiring a conviction sufficiently strong to give them perfect peace of mind.

Even in things that concern health, common sense is applicable to daily life.

It is common sense that will preserve us from excesses, by establishing the equilibrium of the annoyances that result from them, with reference to the doubtful pleasure that they procure.

Thanks to common sense, we shall avoid the weariness of late nights and the danger of giving oneself up to the delights of dissipation.

"It is common sense," says the philosopher, "which forces us at a banquet to raise our eyes to the clock to find out how late it is.

"It is under the inspiration of this great quality of mind that we shall avoid putting to our lips the cup already emptied many times.

"Common sense will reflect upon the mirror of our imagination the specter of the day after the orgy; it will evoke the monster of the headache which works upon the suffering cranium with its claws of steel; and, at some future day, it will show us precocious decrepitude as well as all bodily ills which precede the final decay of those who yield to their passions. It will also impose upon us the performance of duty under the form, which it has adopted for each individual.

"Common sense represents for some the care of public affairs; for others those of the family; for us all the great desire to leave intact to our descendants the name which we have received from our ancestors.

"For some of those still very young, it is like a lover long desired!

"For sages and warriors, it blows the trumpet of glory.

"Finally, common sense is the chosen purpose of every one, courted, demanded, desired or accepted, but *it exists,* and under the penalty of most serious inconveniences it does not permit us to forget its existence."

Coming down from the heights where he allows himself to be transported at times for a brief moment, Yoritomo tells us the part played by common sense with reference to health.

"Common sense" he assures us, "is the wisest physician whom it is possible to consult.

"If we followed its advice, we should avoid the thousand and one little annoyances of illnesses caused by imprudence.

"The choice of clothing would be regulated according to the existing temperature.

"One would avoid the passing at once from extreme heat to extreme cold.

"One would never proffer this stupid reflection: Bah! I shall take care of myself, which impudent people declare when exposing themselves carelessly to take cold.

"We should understand that disease is a cause of unparalleled disorder and discord.

"In addition to the thought of possible sufferings, that of grief for those whom we love, joined to the apprehension of a cessation of social functions, on whose achievement depends our fortune, would suffice to eliminate all idea of imprudence, if we had the habit of allowing common sense to participate in all our actions of daily life.

"To those who walk under its guidance, it manifests itself without ceasing; it dominates all actions without their being compelled to separate themselves from it.

"It is unconsciously that they appeal to common sense and they have no need of making an effort to follow its laws.

"Common sense is the intelligence of instinct."

Lesson VII
Power of Deduction

Before entering the path that relates directly to the intellectual efforts concerning the acquisition of common sense, the Shogun calls our attention to the power of deduction.

"It is only," said he, "where we are sufficiently permeated with all the principles of judgment that we shall be able to think of acquiring this quality, so necessary to the harmony of life.

"The most important of all the mental operations which ought to be practiced by those who desire common sense to reign supreme in all their actions and decisions, is incontestably deduction.

"When the union of ideas, which judgment permits, is made with perception and exactness, there results always an analysis, which, if practiced frequently, will end by becoming almost a mechanical act.

"It is, however, well to study the phases of this analysis, in order to organize them methodically first.

"Later, when the mind shall be sufficiently drilled in this kind of gymnastics, all their movements will be repeated in an almost unconscious way, and deduction, that essential principle of common sense will be self-imposed.

"In order that deductions may be a natural development, the element relating to those which should be the object of judgment should be grouped first.

"The association of statements is an excellent method for it introduces into thought the existence of productive agents.

"We have already spoken of the grouping of thoughts, which is a more synthetic form of that selection.

"Instead of allowing it to be enlarged by touching lightly on all that which is connected with the subject, it is a question, on the contrary, of confining it to the facts relating to only one object.

"These facts should be drawn from the domain of the past; by comparison, they can be brought to the domain of the present in order to be able to associate the former phenomena with those from which it is a question of drawing deductions.

"It is rarely that these latter depend on one decision alone, even when they are presented under the form of a single negation or affirmation.

"Deduction is always the result of many observations, formulated with great exactness, which common sense binds together.

"That which is called a line of action is always suggested by the analysis of the events that were produced under circumstances analogous to those that exist now.

"From the result of these observations, the habit of thinking permits of drawing deductions and common sense concludes the analysis.

"The method of deduction rests upon this.

"One thing being equal to a previous one should produce the same effects.

"If we find ourselves faced by an incident that our memory can assimilate with another incident of the same kind, we must deduce the following chain of reasoning:

"First, the incident of long ago has entailed inevitable consequences.

"Secondly, the incident of today ought to produce the same effects, unless the circumstances which surround it are different.

"It is then a question of analyzing the circumstances and of weighing the causes whose manifestation could determine a disparity in the results.

"We shall interest ourselves first in the surroundings, for thus, as we have said, habits of thought and feeling vary according to the epoch and the environment.

"A comparison will be established between persons or things, in order to be absolutely convinced of their degree of conformity.

"The state of mind in which we were when the previous events were manifested will be considered, and we shall not fail to ascertain plainly the similarity or change of humor at the moment as related to that of the past.

"It is also of importance to observe the state of health, for under the affliction of sickness things assume very easily a hostile aspect.

"It would be wrong to attribute to events judged during an illness the same value that is given to them at this present moment.

"When one is absolutely decided as to the relation of new perceptions and mental representations, one can calculate exactly the degree of comparison.

"The moment will then have arrived to synthesize all the observations and to draw from them the following deductions:

"First, like causes ought, all things being equal, to produce like effects.

"Secondly, the event that is in question will therefore have the same consequences as the previous one, since it is presented under the same conditions.

"Being granted the principle that like causes produce like effects, as I have just affirmed, and that there exist certain incompatibilities between the contingencies of the past and those of today, one must allow that these incompatibilities will produce different results.

"And, after this reasoning, the deductions will be established by constituting a comparison in favor of either the present or past state of things."

But the philosopher, who thinks of everything, has foreseen the case where false ideas have obscured the clearness of the deductions, and he said to us:

"The association of false ideas, if it does not proceed from the difficulty of controlling things, is always in ungovernable opposition to the veracity of the deduction.

"What would be thought of a man of eighty years who, coming back to his country after long absence, said, on seeing the family roof from a distance:

"'When I was twenty years old, in leaving here, it took me twenty minutes to reach the home of my parents, so I shall reach the threshold in twenty minutes.'

"The facts would be exact in principle.

"The distance to be covered would be the same; but legs of eighty years have not the same agility as those of very young people, and in predicting that he will reach the end of his walk in the same number of minutes as he did in the past, the old man would deceive himself most surely.

"If, on the contrary, on reaching the same place he perceived that a new route had been made, and that instead of a roundabout way of approach, as in the past, the house was now in a straight line from the point where he was looking at it, it would be possible to estimate approximately the number of minutes which he could gain on the time employed in the past, by calculating the delay imposed upon him by his age and his infirmities.

"Those to whom deduction is familiar, at times astonish thoughtless persons by the soundness of their judgment.

"A prince drove to his home in the country in a sumptuous equipage.

"He was preceded by a herald and borne in a palanquin by four servants, who were replaced by others at the first signs of fatigue, in order that the speed of the journey should never be slackened.

"As they were mounting, with great difficulty, a zigzag road that led up along the side of a hill, one of these men cried out:

"'Stop,' said he, 'in the name of Buddha, stop!'

"The prince leaned out from the palanquin to ask the cause of this exclamation:

"'My lord,' cried the man, 'if you care to live, tell your porters to stop!'

"The great man shrugged his shoulders and turning toward his master of ceremonies, who was riding at his side, said:

"'See what that man wants.'

"But scarcely had the officer allowed his horse to take a few steps in the direction of the man who had given warning when the palanquin, with the prince and his bearers, rolled down a precipice, opened by the sinking in of the earth.

"They raised them all up very much hurt, and the first action of the prince, who was injured, was to have arrested the one who, according to him, had evoked an evil fate.

"He was led, then and there, to the nearest village and put into a cell.

"The poor man protested.

"'I have only done what was natural,' said he. 'I am going to explain it, but I pray you let me see the prince; I shall not be able to justify myself when he is ill with fever.'

"'What do you mean,' they replied, 'do you prophesy that the prince will have a fever?'

"'He is going to have it.'

"'You see, you are a sorcerer,' said the jailer, 'you make predictions.'

"And then he shut him in prison, to go away and to relate his conversation to them all.

"During this time, they called in a healer who stated that the wounds of the great nobleman were not mortal in themselves, but that the fever which had declared itself could become dangerous.

"After long months, the prince was cured.

"During this time the poor man languished in his prison, from whence he was only taken to appear before the judges.

"Accused of sorcery and of using black magic, he explained very simply that he had foreseen the danger, because in raising his eyes he had noticed that the part of the ground over which the herald had passed was sinking, and that he had drawn the following conclusions:

"The earth seemed to have only a medium thickness.

"Under the feet of the herald he had seen it crumble and fall in.

"He had deduced from this that a weight five times as heavy added to that of the palanquin, would not fail to produce a landslide.

"As to the prediction concerning the fever, it was based on what he had seen when in the war.

"He had then observed that every wound is always followed by a disposition to fever; he therefore could not fail to deduce that the serious contusions occasioned by the fall of the prince would produce the inevitable consequences.

"The judge was very much impressed with the perspicacity of this man; not only did he give him his liberty, but he engaged him in his personal service and in due time enabled him to make his fortune."

We do not wish to affirm—anymore than Yoritomo, for that matter—that fortunate deductions are always so magnificently rewarded, as were those of this man.

However, without the causes being so striking, many people have owed their fortune to, the faculty that they possessed of deducing results where the analogy of the past circumstances suggested to them what would happen.

He warns us against the propensity that we have of too easily avoiding a conclusion, which does not accord with our desires.

"Too many people," said he, "wish to undertake to make deductions by eliminating the elements which deprive them of a desired decision.

"They do not fail either to exaggerate the reasons which plead in favor of this decision; also we see many persons suffer from reasoning, instead of feeling the good effects of it."

Those who cultivate common sense will never fall into this error, for they will have no difficulty in convincing themselves that by acting thus they do not deceive any one except themselves.

By glossing over truth in order to weaken the logical consequences of deductions they are the first to be the victims of this childish trick.

That which is called false deduction is rarely taught save the desire to escape a resolution that a just appraisement would not fail to dictate.

It might be, also, that this twisting of judgment comes from a person having been, in some past time, subjected to unfortunate influences.

By devoting oneself to the evolution of thought, of which we have already spoken when presenting the symbolical fan, and above all, by adopting the precepts which, following the method of Yoritomo, we are going to develop in the following lessons, we shall certainly succeed in checking the errors of false reasoning.

"The important thing," said he "is not to let wander the thought, which, after resting for a moment on the subject with which we are concerned and after touching lightly on ideas of a similar character, begins to stray very far from its basic principles.

"Have you noted the flight of certain birds?

"They commence by gathering at one point, then they describe a series of circles around this point, at first very small, but whose circumference enlarges at every sweep.

"Little by little the central point is abandoned, they no longer approach it, and disappear in the sky, drawn by their fancy toward another point which they will leave very soon.

"The thoughts of one who does not know how to gather them together and to concentrate them are like these birds.

"They start from a central point, and then spread out, at first without getting far from this center, but soon they lose sight of it and fly toward a totally different subject that a mental representation has just produced.

"And this lasts until the moment when, in a sudden movement, the first one is conscious of this wandering tendency.

"But it is often too late to bring back these wanderers to the initial idea, for, in the course of their circuits, they have brushed against a hundred others, which are confounded with the first, weaken it, and take away its exact proportions.

"The great stumbling-block again is that of becoming lost in the details whose multiplicity prevents us from discerning their complete function in the act of practicing deduction.

"It is better, in the case where our perception finds itself assailed by the multitude of these details, to proceed by the process of elimination, in order not to become involved in useless and lazy efforts.

"In this case we must act like a man who must determine the color of a material at a distance where the tiny designs stand out in a relief of white on a background of black.

"Suppose that he is placed at a distance too great to perceive this detail.

"What should he do to be able to give the best possible description?

"He will proceed by elimination.

"The material is neither red nor green; orange and violet must be set aside, as well as all the subordinate shades.

"It has a dull appearance, hence, it is gray; unless . . . And here mental activity comes into play and will suggest to him that gray is composed of black and white.

"He will then be sure to form a judgment that will not be spoiled by falsity, if he declares that the material is a mixture of black and white.

"Later, by drawing nearer, he will be able to analyze the designs and to convince himself, of their respective form and color, but by deducing that the material was made up of the mixture of two colors he will have come as near as possible to the truth.

"Deduction never prejudges; it is based on facts; only on things accomplished; it unfolds the teaching that we ought to obtain as a result."

Again the Shogun recommends to us the union of thoughts and the continuous examination of past incidents in the practice of deductions.

"If on entering a room," said he, "we are at times confused, it happens also that we correct this impression after a more attentive examination.

"The gilding is of inferior quality; the materials are of cotton, the paintings ordinary, and the matting coarse.

"At first sight we should have deduced, judging from appearances, that the possessor of this house was a very rich man, but a second examination will cause us to discover embarrassment and anxiety.

"It is the same with all decisions that we must make.

"Before devoting ourselves to deductions inspired by the general aspect of things, it is well to examine them one by one and to discover their defects or recognize their good qualities.

"We shall be able thus to acquire that penetration of mind whose development, by leading us toward wise deductions, will bring us to the discovery of the truth."

Lesson VIII

How to Acquire Common Sense

Common Sense is a science, whatever may be said; according to Yoritomo, it does not blossom naturally in the human mind; it demands cultivation, and the art of reasoning is acquired like all the faculties which go to make up moral equilibrium.

"This quality," said the philosopher "is obscure and intangible.

"Like the air we breathe, it is necessary to our existence; it surrounds us, envelops us, and is indispensable to the harmony of our mental life.

"To acquire this precious gift, many conditions are obligatory, the principal ones being:

"Sincerity of perception.

"Art of the situation.

"Attention.

"Approximation.

"Experience.

"Comparison.

"Analysis.

"Synthesis.

"Destination.

"Direction.

"And lastly, the putting of the question.

"It is very clear that without exactness of perception we could not pretend to judge justly; it would then be impossible for us to hear the voice of common sense, if we did not strive to develop it.

"Perception is usually combined with what they call in philosophical language *adaptation*.

"Otherwise it is difficult, when recognizing a sensation, not to attribute it at once to the sentiment that animated it at the time of its manifestation.

"The first condition, then, in the acquiring of common sense is to maintain perfection in all its pristine exactness, by abstracting the contingencies which could influence us.

"If we do not endeavor to separate from our true selves the suggestions of sense-consciousness, we shall reach the point where *perception* is transformed into *conception*, that is to say, we shall no longer obtain reality alone, but a modified reality.

"With regard to perception, if we understand its truthfulness, it will be a question for reawakening it, of placing ourselves mentally in the environment where it was produced, and of awakening the memory, so as to be able to distinguish, without mistake, the limits within which it is narrowly confined.

"The art of situation consists in reproducing, mentally past facts, allowing for the influence of the surroundings at that time, as compared with the present environment.

"One must not fail to think about the influences to which one has been subjected since this time.

"It is possible that life during its development in the aspirant to common sense may have changed the direction of his first conceptions either by conversation or by reading or by the reproduction of diverse narrations.

"It would then be a lack of common sense to base an exact recollection of former incidents on the recent state of being of the soul, without seeking to reproduce the state of mind in which one was at the epoch when those incidents occurred.

"Activity of mind, stimulated to the utmost, is able to give a color to preceding impressions, which they never have had, and, in this case again; the recollection will be marred by inexactness.

"The art of situation requires the strictest application and on this account it is a valuable factor in the acquirement of common sense.

"Attention vitalizes our activity in order to accelerate the development of a definite purpose toward which it can direct its energy.

"It could be analyzed as follows:

"First, to see;

"Secondly, to hear.

"The functions of the other senses come afterward, and their susceptibility can attract our attention to the sensations that they give us, such as the sense of smell, of touch, of taste.

"These purely physical sensations possess, however, a moral signification, from which we are permitted to make valuable deductions.

The first two have three distinct phases:

"First degree, to see;

"Second degree, to look;

"Third degree, to observe.

"If we see a material, its color strikes us first and we say: I have seen a red or yellow material, and this will be all.

"Applying ourselves more closely, we *look at* it and we define the peculiarities of the color. We say: it is bright red or dark red.

"In observing it we determine to what use it is destined.

"The eye is attracted by the color, the movement, the form, the number, and the duration.

"We have just spoken of the color.

"The movement is personified by a series of gestures that people make or by a series of changes to which they subject things.

"The form is represented by the different outlines; the number by their quantity; the duration by their length; for example, one will judge of the length of time it takes to walk a road by seeing the length of it.

"The act of listening is divided into three degrees: the first degree, to hear; the second degree, to recognize, and the third degree, to reflect. If when walking in the country we hear a dog bark we perceive first a sound: this is the act of hearing. We will distinguish that this sound is produced by the barking of a dog; this is the act of understanding.

"Reflection will lead us then to think that a house or a human being is near, for a dog rarely goes alone.

"If the things which are presented to our sight are complex, those which strike our ears are summed up in one word, sound, which has only one definition, the quality of the sound.

"Then follow the innumerable categories of sound that we distinguish only by means of comprehension and reflection, rendered so instinctive by habit that we may call them automatic, so far as those which relate to familiar sounds.

"The example which we have just given is a proof of this fact.

"Let us add that this habit develops each sensitive faculty to its highest degree.

"The inhabitants of the country can distinguish each species of bird by listening to his song; and the hermits, the wanderers, those who live with society on a perpetual war footing, perceive sounds which would not strike the ears of civilized people.

"Approximation is also one of the stones by whose aid we construct the edifice of common sense.

"Concerning the calculations of probabilities, the application of approximation will allow us to estimate the capacity or the probable duration of things.

"We can not say positively whether a person will live a definite number of years but we can affirm that he or she will never live to the age of two hundred.

"There are, for approbation, certain known limits which serve as a basis for the construction of reasoning, inspired by common sense.

"It can be affirmed, in a positive way, that, if the trunk of a tree were floating easily, without sinking to the bottom of the water, it would not float the same if thirty people were to ride astride of it.

"The initial weight of the tree permits it to maintain itself on the surface; but if it be increased to an exaggerated total, we can, without hesitation, calculate indirectly the moment when it will disappear, dragging with it the imprudent people who trusted themselves to it.

"Everything in life is a question of approximation.

"The house which is built for a human will be far larger than the kennel, destined to shelter a dog, because the proportions have been calculated, by approximation, according to the relative difference between the stature of the human and canine species.

"Clothing is also suited to the temperature.

"One naturally thinks that, below a certain degree of cold, it is necessary to change light clothes for those made of thicker material.

"As with the majority of the constructive elements of common sense, approximation is always based on experience.

"It draws its conclusions from the knowledge of known limitations, whose affirmation serves as a basis for the argument that determines deduction in a most exact manner.

"Experience itself depends on memory, which permits us to recall facts and to draw reasonable conclusions from them."

The Shogun does not fail to draw our attention to the difference between experience and experimentation.

"This last," said he, "only serves to incite the manifestation of the first.

"It consists of determining the production of a phenomenon whose existence will aid us in establishing the underlying principles of an observation that interprets the event.

"That is what is called experience.

"Comparison is a mental operation which permits us to bring things that we desire to understand to a certain point.

"It is comparison that has divided time according to periods, which the moon follows during its entire length.

"It is by comparing their different aspects and by calculating the duration of their transformations, that we have been able to divide time as we do in all the countries of the world.

"The science of numbers is also born of comparison, which has been established between the quantities that they represent.

"This is the art of calculating the differences existing between each thing, by determining the relativeness of their respective proportions.

"Comparison acts on the mind automatically, as a rule.

"It is indispensable to the cultivation of common sense, for it furnishes the means of judging with full knowledge of all the circumstances.

"Analysis is an operation, which consists of separating each detail from the whole and of examining these details separately, without losing sight of their relationship to the central element.

"Analysis of the same object, while being scrupulously exact, can, however, differ materially in its application, according to the way that the object is related to this or that group of circumstances.

"There are, however, immutable things.

"For example: the letters of the alphabet, the elementary sounds, and the colors.

"It suffices to quote only these three elements; one can easily understand that the most elaborate manuscript is composed of only a definite number of letters always repeating themselves, whose juxtaposition forms phrases, then chapters, and finally the complete work.

"Music is composed only of seven sounds whose different combinations produce an infinite variety of melodies.

"Elementary colors are only three in number.

"All the others gravitate around them.

"Therefore, these same letters, these same notes, these same colors, according to their amalgamation, can change in aspect and cooperate in the production of different effects.

"The same letters can express, according to the order in which they are placed, terror or confidence, joy or grief.

"The same is true of notes and colors.

"Common sense ought then, considering these rules, to know how to analyze all the details and, having done this, to coordinate and to classify them, in order to distinguish them easily.

"Coordination and classification form an integral part of common sense."

Yoritomo, who delights in reducing the most complex questions to examples of the rarest simplicity, says to us:

"I am supposing that one person says to another, I have just seen a nightingale. The interlocutors, as well as those who mechanically register this fact, without thinking, give themselves up to analysis and to coordination which always precedes synthesis.

"Without being aware of this mental action, their minds will be occupied first with the operations of perception then of classification.

"This nightingale was of a species which places it in a certain type of bird that sings beautifully.

"It is always thus that common sense proceeds, its principal merit being to know how to unite present perceptions with those previously recognized, then to understand how to coordinate them so as to be able to group them concretely, that is to say, to synthesize them. They did not hear the nightingale sing, but deduced that as it was of that species it would sing beautifully.

"Destination is defined as the purpose or object, born of deduction and of classification.

"Destination does not permit of losing sight of the end that is proposed.

"It allows the consideration of the purpose to predominate always, and directs all actions toward this purpose, these actions being absolutely the demonstrations of this unique thought.

"Habits, acquired in view of certain realizations, ought to be dropped from the moment the purpose is accomplished, or that it is weakened."

It is by absolutely perpetuating those habits, whose pretext has disappeared, that one sees the achievement of certain actions that have been roughly handled by common sense.

"There are," again says the philosopher, "certain customs, whose origin it is impossible to remember; at the time of their birth, they were engendered by necessity, but even though their purpose be obliterated, tradition has preserved them in spite of everything, and those who observe them do not take into consideration their absurdity.

"People of common sense refrain from lending themselves to these useless practices, or, if they consent to allow them a place in their thoughts it is that they attribute to them some reason for existence, either practical or sentimental."

Direction is indicated by circumstances, by environment, or by necessity.

There is direction of resolutions as well as direction of a journey; it is necessary, from the beginning, to consider well the choice of a good route, after having done everything possible to discriminate carefully between it and all other routes proposed.

It happens, however, that the way leads also through the crossroads; it is even indispensable to leave the shortcuts in order to trace the outline of the obstacles.

Direction is, then, an important factor in the acquiring of common sense.

The putting of the question takes its character from comparison, from experience, and principally from approximation; but it is in itself a synthesis of all the elements that compose common sense.

Those who wish to acquire common sense should be impregnated with all that has preceded, then they will discipline themselves, so as to be able to judge, by themselves, of the degree of reason which they have the right to assume.

They will begin by evoking some subject, comparing its visual forms with those forms which they understand the best, in other words, to the perceptions which are the most familiar to them.

If it concerns a question to be solved, they will try to recall some similar subject, and establish harmony, by making them both relative to a common antecedent.

Yoritomo advises choosing simple thoughts for the beginning.

"One will say, for example:

"Such a substance is a poison; the seeds of this fruit contain a weak dose of it; these seeds could then become a dangerous food, if one absorbed a considerable quantity.

"Common sense will thus indicate a certain abstaining from eating of it.

"Then one may extend his argument to things of a greater importance, but taking great care to keep within the narrow limits of rudimentary logic.

"One must be impregnated with this principle:

"Two things equal to a third demand an affirmative judgment or decision.

"In the opposite case the negative deduction is enjoined.

"It is by deductions from the most ordinary facts that one succeeds in making common sense intervene automatically in all our judgments.

"What would be thought of a wanderer who, finding himself in a forest at the time of a violent storm, would reason as follows:

"First, the high summits attract lightning;

"Secondly: Here is a giant tree;

"Thirdly: I am going to take refuge there.

"Then it is that common sense demands that the three propositions be stated as follows:

"First, high summits attract lightning;

"Secondly, here is a giant tree;

"Thirdly, I am going to avoid its proximity because it will surely be dangerous.

"If he acted otherwise; if, in spite of his knowledge of the danger, he took shelter under the branches of the gigantic tree, exposing himself to be struck by lightning, one could, in this case, only reproach him with imprudence and lay the blame to the lack of common sense which allowed him to perform the act that logic condemned."

Now the old Nippon speaks to us of the means to employ, that we may avoid pronouncing too hasty judgments, which are always, of necessity, weakened by a too great indulgence for ourselves and at the same time too great a severity for others.

"I was walking one day," said he, "on the shores of a lake, when I discovered a man sitting at the foot of a bamboo tree, in an attitude of the greatest despair.

"Approaching him, I asked him the cause of his grief.

"'Alas!' said he to me, 'the gods are against me; everything which I undertake fails, and all evils crush me.

"'After the one which has just befallen me only one course of action is left to me, to throw myself in the lake. But I am young, and I am weeping for myself before resolving to take such a step.'

"And he related to me how, after many attempts without success, he had at last gained a certain sum of money, the loss of which he had just experienced.

"'In what way did you lose it?' I asked him.

"'I put it in this bag.'

"'Has some one stolen it?'

"'No, it has slipped through this rent.'

"And he showed me a bag, whose ragged condition confirmed, and at the same time illustrated his statement.

"'Listen,' said I, sitting down beside him, 'you are simply devoid of common sense, by invoking the hatred of the gods! You alone are the cause of your present misery.'

"'If you had simply reasoned before placing your money in this bag, this would not have happened to you.'

"And as he opened his eyes wide:

"'You would have thought this,' I resumed:

"'The material, very much worn, is incapable of standing any weight without tearing.

"'Now, the money which I possess is heavy, my bag is worn out.

"'I shall not, therefore, put my money in this bag or, at least, I shall take care to line it beforehand with a solid piece of leather.

"'From this moment,' I proceeded, 'there only remains one thing for you to do, always consult common sense before coming to any conclusion, and you will always succeed.'

"'As for your opinion concerning the hatred of the gods for you, if you will once more call common sense to your assistance you will reason as follows:

"'Gracious divinities protect only wise people.'

"'Now, I have acted like a fool.'

"'It is, therefore, natural that they should turn away from me.'

"How many useless imprecations would be avoided," adds the Shogun, "if it were given to us to know how to employ the arguments which common sense dictates, in order to distribute the weight of the mistakes committed among those who deserve the burden, without, at the same time, forgetting to assume our own share of the responsibility if we have erred.

"Nothing is more sterile than regrets or reproaches, when they do not carry with them the resolution never again to fall into the same error."

Afterward the philosopher demonstrates to us the necessity of abstracting all personality from the exercises that combine for the attainment of common sense.

"There is," said he, "an obstacle against which all stupid people stumble; it is the act of reasoning under the influence of passion.

"Those *who* have not decided to renounce this method of arguing will never be able to give a just decision.

"There are self-evident facts, *which* certain people refuse to admit, because this statement of the truth offends their sympathies or impedes their hatreds, and they force themselves to deny the evidence, hoping thus to deceive others regarding it.

"But truth is always the strongest and they soon become the solitary dupes of their own willful blindness.

"People with common sense know how to recognize falsehood wherever they meet it; they knows how vain it is to conceal a positive fact and also how dangerous it is to deceive oneself, a peril which increases in power, in proportion to the effort made to ignore it.

"They do not wish to imitate those pusillanimous people who prefer to live in the agony of doubt rather than to look misfortunes in the face. If you are determined to acquire common sense, use the following argument:

"Doubt is a conflict between two conclusions.

"So long as it exists it is impossible to adopt either.

"Serenity is unknown to those whom doubt attacks.

"To obtain peace, it is necessary to become enlightened.

"However, it is wise always to foresee the least happy issue and to prepare to support the consequences.

"Those who think thus will be stronger than adversity and will know how to struggle with misfortune without allowing it to master them."

It is in these terms that Yoritomo initiates us into what he calls the mechanism of common sense, in other words the art of acquiring by the simplest reasoning this quality dull as iron, but, like it, also solid and durable.

Lesson IX
Common Sense and Action

These qualities are two relatives very near of kin; but, just for this reason, they must not be confounded.

While common sense is applied to all the circumstances of life, practical sense is applicable to useful things.

Common sense admits a very subtle logic that is, at times, a little complex.

Practical sense starts from one point only—material conveniences.

It is possible for this sense to be spoiled by egotism, if common sense does not come to its assistance.

It is by applying the discipline of reasoning to practical sense that it modifies simple sense perception by urging it to ally itself with logic, which unites thought to sentiment and reason.

"The association of common sense and practical sense is necessary," says Yoritomo, "in order to produce new forms, at the same time restraining the imagination within the limits of the most exact deductions and of the most impartial judgment."

Science is, in reality, a sort of common sense to which the rules of reasoning are applied, and is supported by arguments which practical sense directs into productive channels.

That which is called great common sense is none other than a quality with which people are endowed who show great mental equilibrium whenever it is a question of resolving material problems.

These people are generally persons of humble position, whose physical organism has been developed without paying much attention to their intellectual education; they are, in fact, perfect candidates for the attainment of common sense, without having been educated to this end.

Their aptitude results from a constant habit of reflection that, rendering their attention very keen, has permitted them to observe the most minute details; therefore they can form correct conclusions, when it is a question of things that are familiar to them.

Peasants, who have been taught by nature, will be more skilled in prophesying about the weather than others.

They will also know how to assign a limit to the daily working hours, at the same time stating the maximum time that one can give without developing repulsion, which follows excesses of all kinds.

In their thought, very simple, but very direct, will be formulated this perfect reasoning:

Health is the first of all blessings, since without it we are incapable of appreciating the other joys of life.

If we compromise this possession we shall be insensible to all others.

It is, therefore, indispensable that we should measure our efforts, for, admitting that a certain exaggerated labor may bring us a fortune, we shall not know how to enjoy it if illness accompanies it.

This is the logic that is called practical sense.

Yoritomo continues, saying that there is a very close connection between the faculty of judging and that of deducing.

"Practical sense, allied to commonsense, comes to the assistance of the latter, when it is tempted to reject the chain of analogy, whose representation too often draws one far from the initial subject.

"It facilitates coordination, clearness, and precision of thought.

"It knows how to consider contingencies, and never fails to have a clear understanding of relative questions."

To illustrate his theory, he cites us an example which many of our young contemporaries would do well to remember.

"There was," said he, "in the village of Fu-Isher, a literary man, who wrote beautiful poems.

"He lived in great solitude, and no one would have heard of his existence if it had not been that my master, Lang-Ho, while walking in the woods one day, was attracted by the harmonious sounds of poetry, which this young man was reciting, without thinking that he had any other listeners than the birds of the forest.

"Lang-Ho made himself known to him and began to question him.

"He learned that he did not lack ambition, but, being poor, and having no means of approaching those who would have been able to patronize him, he was singing of nature for his own pleasure, waiting patiently until he should be able to influence the powerful ones of the earth to share his appreciation.

"Lang-Ho, touched by his youth and his ardor, pointed out to him the dwelling of a prince, a patron of the arts, and, at the same time, told him how he ought to address the nobleman, assuring him that the fact of his being a messenger from a friend of the prince would open the doors of the palace to him.

"The next day the young poet presented himself at the home of the great lord, who, knowing that he had been sent by Lang-Ho, received him in spite of the fact that he was suffering intensely from a violent headache.

"He learned from the young man that he was a poet and treated him with great consideration, making him understand, however, that all sustained mental effort was insupportable to him on that day.

"But the poet, not paying attention to the prince's expressed desire, unrolled his manuscripts and began reading an interminable ode without noticing the signs of impatience shown by his august hearer.

"He did not have the pleasure of finishing it.

"The prince, seeing that the reader did not understand his importunity, struck a gong and ordered the servant who appeared to conduct the young man out of his presence.

"Later, he declared to Lang-Ho that his *protégé* had no talent at all, and reprimanded him severely for having sent the poet to the palace.

"But my master did not like to be thus criticized.

"So, a little while after that, one day, when that same prince was in an agreeable frame of mind, Lang-Ho invited him to the reading of one of his works.

"The nobleman declared that he had never heard anything more beautiful.

"'That is true,' said Lang-Ho, 'but you ought to have said this the first time you heard it.'

"And he revealed to the prince that these verses were those of the young man whom he had judged so harshly."

From this story two lessons may be drawn:

The first is that if common sense indicates that judgment should not change from scorn to enthusiasm, when it is a question of the same object, practical sense insists that one should be certain of impartiality of judgment, by avoiding the influence of questions which relate to environment and surrounding circumstances.

The second concerns opportunity.

We have already had occasion to say how much some things, which seem desirable at certain times, are questionable when the situation changes.

Bad humor creates ill will; therefore it is abominably stupid to provoke the manifestation of the second when one has proved the existence of the first.

In order that there may be a connection between the faculty of judgment and that of deduction, it is essential that nothing should be allowed to interpose itself between these two phases of the argument.

Harmony between all judgments is founded on common sense, but it is practical common sense, which indicates this harmony with precision.

It is also practical common sense that serves as a guide to orators who wish to impress their audiences.

They will endeavor first to choose a subject that will interest those who listen to them.

In this endeavor they ought, above all, to consult opportunity.

As we have remarked on many occasions, the Shogun expresses theories on this subject, to which the people of the twenty-first century could not give too much earnest consideration.

"There are," said he, "social questions, as, for example, dress and custom.

"With time, opinions change, as do forms and manners, and this is quite reasonable.

"The progress of science by ameliorating the general conditions of existence, introduces a need created by civilization which rejects barbarous customs; the mentality of a warrior is not that of an agriculturist. People who think about making their possessions productive do not have the same inclinations as those whose life is devoted to conquest, and the sweetness of living in serenity, by modifying the aspirations, metamorphoses all things.

"In order to lead attention in the direction which is governed by reason, it is indispensable for the orators that they should expound a subject whose interpretation will satisfy the demand of opportunity, which influences every brain.

"Practical sense will make them take care to speak only of things that they have studied thoroughly.

"It will induce them to expound their theory in such a way that their hearers will have to make no effort to assimilate it.

"That which is not understood is easily criticized, and practical sense would prevent orators from attempting to establish any arguments whose premises would offend common sense.

"They would be certain of failure in such a case.

"Their efforts will be limited, then, to evoking common sense, by employing practical sense, so far as what refers to the application of principles which they desire to apply successfully."

Yoritomo recommends this affiliation for that which concerns the struggle against superstition.

"Superstition," he says, "offends practical sense as well as common sense, for it rests on an erroneous analysis.

"Its foundation is always an observation marred by falsity, establishing an association between two facts that have nothing in common.

"There are people who, when they reach the threshold of their home and they perceive a certain bird will turn around and then come back later to reenter their home. There are others who believe that they are threatened with death if they meet a black cat."

Without going back to the days of Yoritomo, we shall find just as many people today who are the victims of superstitions concerning certain facts, which are only the observance of customs fallen into disuse, and whose practice has been perpetuated through the ages, although, as we have said in the preceding chapter, the purpose of the custom has disappeared, but the custom itself has not been forgotten.

It is in this way that the origin of the superstition concerning salt dates back to the time of the Romans, who (while at variance with the principles of contemporary agriculture) sowed salt in the fields of their enemies and thought that by so doing they would make them sterile.

To that far-distant epoch can be traced the origin of the superstition concerning the spilling of salt.

Whatever may have been its cause, superstition is the enemy of common sense, for, when it does not originate in an abolished custom, it is the product of a personal impression, associating two ideas absolutely unconnected.

"Practical sense," Yoritomo continues, "is a most valuable talent to cultivate, for it prevents our judging from appearances.

"Frivolous minds are always inclined to draw conclusions from passing impressions; they adopt neither foresight, nor precaution, nor approximation.

"There are people who will condemn a country as utterly unattractive, because they happened to have visited it under unfavorable circumstances.

"Others, without considering what a country has previously produced and that at present the grain has not been planted, will declare unfertile the soil that has been unfilled for some months.

"On the other hand, if they visit a house on a sunny day, it would be impossible for them to associate it with the idea of rain.

"It would be most difficult to make these people alter their judgment, prematurely formed, and, in spite of the most authoritative assertions and the most self-evident proofs, their initial idea will dominate all those which one would like to instill into their minds.

"One moment would, however, suffice for reason to convince them that the variations of atmosphere and the conditions of cultivation can modify the aspect of a country, of a field, and of a house, to the extent of giving them an appearance totally different from the one which they seemed to have.

"But those who judge by appearances never rejoice in the possession of that faculty which may be called reason in imagination.

"This is a gift, developed by practical sense and which common sense happily directs in right channels.

"Those who are endowed with this faculty can, with the help of reasoning, and by means of thought, build up a future reality based on a judgment whose affirmation admits of no doubt.

"It is not a question of hypothesis, no matter how well founded it is.

"Experience, in this case, is united with deduction to form a preconceived but certain idea.

"By cultivating practical sense, we shall escape the danger of idealization which, with people of unbalanced mentality, often sheds an artificial light upon the picture."

There is still another point to which Yoritomo calls our attention, in order to encourage us to cultivate the twin reasoning powers whose advantages we are trying to commend in this chapter:

"Practical sense," he says, "sometimes puts common sense apparently in the wrong, while acting, however, without the inspiration of the latter."

Lesson X

The Most Thorough Business Manager

One of the principle advantages of common sense is that it protects the person who is gifted with it from hazardous enterprises, the risky character of which is perceived.

Only to risk when possessing perfect knowledge of a subject is the sure means of never being drawn into a transaction by illusory hopes.

An exact conception of things is more indispensable to perfect success than a thousand other more brilliant but less substantial gifts.

"However," says Yoritomo, "in order to make success our own, it is not sufficient to have the knowledge of *things*, one must above all know oneself.

"On the great world stage, each one occupies a place which at the start may not always be in the first rank.

"Nevertheless, work, intelligence directness of thought and, above all, common sense, can exert a positive influence on the future superiority of the situation.

"Before everything else, it is indispensable that we should never delude ourselves about the position which we occupy.

"To define it exactly, one should call to mind the wise adage that says: Know thyself.

"But this knowledge is rare.

"Presumptuous persons readily imagine that they attract the eyes of every one, even if they be in the last rank.

"Timid persons will hide themselves behind others and, notwithstanding; they are very much aggrieved not to be seen.

"Ambitious persons push away the troublesome ones, in order that they themselves may get the first places.

"Lazy persons just let them do it.

"Irresolute persons hesitate before sitting down in vacant places and are consumed with regrets from the time they perceive that others, better prepared, take possession of them; the more so as they no longer get back their own, for, during their hesitation, another has seated himself there.

"Enthusiasts fight to reach the first rank, but are so fatigued by their violent struggles that they fall, tired out, before they have attained their object.

"Obstinate people persist in coveting inaccessible places and spend strength without results, which they might have employed more judiciously.

"People of common sense are the only ones who experience no nervous tension because of this struggle.

"They calculate their chances, compute the time, do not disturb themselves uselessly, and never abandon their present position until they have a firm grasp on the following place.

"They do not seek to occupy a rank which their knowledge would not permit them to keep; they draw on that faculty with which they are gifted to learn the science of true proportion.

"They do not meddle in endeavors to reform laws; they submit to them, by learning how to adapt them to their needs, and respect them by seeking to subordinate their opinion to the principle on which they are based.

"Persons who have no common sense are the only ones to revolt against the laws of the country where they live.

"The wise man will recognize that they have been enacted to protect him and that to be opposed to their observance would be acting as an enemy to oneself."

However, people will say, if laws are so impeccable in their right to authority, how is it that their interpretation leads so often to disputes?

It is easy to reply that lawsuits are rarely instituted by people of common sense; they leave this burden to people of evil intent, who imagine thus to make a doubtful cause triumph.

It must be conceded that this means succeeds at times with them, when they are dealing with timid or irresolute persons; but those who have contracted the habit of reasoning, and who never undertake anything without consulting common sense, will never allow themselves to be drawn into the bypaths of sophistry.

If they are forced to enter there temporarily, in order to pursue the adversary, who has hidden himself there, they will leave these paths as soon as necessity does not force them to remain there longer and with delight regain the broad road of rectitude.

A few pages further on we find a reflection that the Shogun, always faithful to his principles of high morality, specially addresses to those who make a profession of humility.

"Obedience," he says, "ought to be considered as a means; but, for the one who wishes to succeed; in no sense can it be honored as a virtue.

"If it be a question of submission to law, it is nothing else but the performance of a strict duty; this is a kind of compact which people of common sense conclude with society, to which they promise their support for the maintenance of a protection from which they will be the first to benefit.

"This obedience might be set down as selfishness were it not endorsed by common sense.

"There are people, it is true, who, even although wishing to support their neighbor when called upon to do so by the law, seek to evade this duty if left to themselves.

"These are pirates who have broken completely not only with the spirit of equity, but also with simple common sense.

"It is always foolish to set the example of insubordination, for, if it were followed, it would not be long before general disorder would appear.

"Some men were sitting one day on the edge of an inlet and were trying with a net to catch fish, whose playful movements the men were following through the limpid water.

"According to their character, their perseverance, their cleverness, and the ingenuity of the means employed, they caught a proportionate number of fish; but even those who caught the least had one or two.

"This success encouraged them, and they began again in good earnest, each one in his own way, when a stranger appeared. He was armed with a long branch of a tree, which he plunged in the pond, touching the bottom and stirring up the mud, which, as it scattered, rose to the surface of the water.

"The limpidity of the water was immediately changed; one could no longer see the fish, and the fishermen decided to discontinue their sport.

"But the man only laughed at their discomfiture and, brandishing a large net, he threw it in his turn, chaffing them at the patient cunning by which they had, he said, taken such a poor haul.

"He brought up some fish, it is true, but at each haul he was obliged to lose so much time in removing the impurities, the debris, and the weeds of all kinds from the net that very soon the fishermen had the satisfaction of seeing him punished for his mean conduct.

"What he took was scarcely more than what the smartest among them had taken, and his net, filthy from the mud, torn by the roots that he was unable to avoid, was soon good for nothing."

Might it not be from this fable that we have taken the expression, "to fish in troubled waters," of which without a doubt the good Yoritomo furnished the origin many, many centuries ago?

His prophetic mind is unveiled again in the following advice that not a business manager of the twenty-first century would reject.

"Common sense," he says, "when it is a question of the relations of people as to what concerns business or society, ought to adopt the characteristic of that animal called the chameleon.

"Its natural color is dull, but it has the gift of reflecting the color of the objects on which it rests.

"Near a leaf, it takes the tint of hope.

"On a lotus, it is glorified with the blue of the sky.

"Is this to say that its nature changes to the point of modifying its natural color?

"No; it does not cease to possess that which recalls the color of the ground, and the ephemeral color that it appropriates is only a semblance, in order that he may be more easily mistaken for the objects themselves.

"People who boast of possessing common sense, although preserving their personality, ought not to fail, if they wants to succeed, to reflect that of the person whom they wish to aid them in succeeding."

Let it not be understood for a moment, that we advise any one to act contrary to the impulses of justice.

But cleverness is a part of common sense in business, and assimilation is essential to success.

It is not necessary to abandon one's convictions in order to reflect principles, which, without contradicting them, give them a favorable color.

Common sense can remain intact and be differently colored, according as it is applied to the arts, politics, or science.

It would not deserve its name if it did not know how to yield to circumstances, in order to adorn the momentary caprice with flowers of reason.

In the primitive ages, common sense consisted in keeping oneself in a perpetual state of defense; attack was also at times prescribed, by virtue of the principle that it is pernicious to allow one's rights to be imperiled.

Attack was also at times a form of repression.

It was also a lesson in obedience and a reminder not to misunderstand individual rights.

In later times, common sense served to make the advantages of harmony appreciated.

It directed the descendants of peoples exclusively warlike toward the secret place where science unfolds itself to the gaze of the vulgar; then it taught them to provide for their existence by working.

It has demonstrated to them the necessity of reflection, by inciting them to model their present course of life on the lessons that come from the past.

It has given them the means to evoke it easily and effectively.

It has injected into their veins the calmness which permits them to draw just conclusions and to adopt toward preceding reasoning the attitude of absolute neutrality, without which all former presentiments are marred by error.

Each epoch was, for common sense, an opportunity to manifest itself differently.

At the moment when poetry was highly honored, it would have been unreasonable to have ignored it, for the bards excited great enthusiasm by their songs, which gave birth to heroes.

And now, imbued with the principles which in his day might be taken to represent what we today call advanced ideas, Yoritomo continues:

"Common sense can, then, without renouncing its devotion to truth, take various forms or shades for the truth of yesterday is not always the truth of today.

"The gods of the past are considered simply, as idols in our day and the virtues of the distant past would be, at present, moral defects which would prevent us from winning the battle of life, whose ideal is *The Best* for which all the faculties should strive."

The Shogun also touches lightly on a subject which, already discussed in his time, has become, in our day, a burning truth; it is a question of a fault, which in the world of practical life and in that of business can cause considerable injury to those who allow it to be implanted in them.

We refer to that tendency which has been adorned or rather branded successively with the names of hypochondria, pessimism, and lastly neurasthenia, an appellation that comprises all kinds of nervous diseases, the characteristic of which is incurable melancholy.

"There are people," he says, "who are afflicted with a special color-blindness.

"Everything they look at assumes immediately to their eyes the most somber hues.

"They see in a flower only the germ of dry rot; the most ideal beauty appears to them only like the negligible covering of some hideous skeleton.

"However, they hang on to this life which they do not cease to calumniate, and people of common sense are rarely found who will try to reason with them from a common-sense stand-point.

"'Since life is so insupportable to you, why do you impose upon yourself the obligation to struggle with it?

"'Only insane people try to prolong their sojourn in a place where they suffer martyrdom.'

"It is true that when, perchance, this argument is placed before them, they do not fail to reply by invoking the shame of desertion.

"'Well, is not then the interest of the struggle to which we are subjected a sufficient attraction to keep us at our post?'"

And, always enamored with the doctrine, which we are now assiduously maintaining, he concludes:

"Common sense is, at times, the unfolding of a magnificent force which incites us to attune our environment to actualities.

"One must not, however, fall into excess and draw a huge sword to pierce the clouds, which obscure the sun.

"If struggle is praiseworthy when we have to face a real enemy, it becomes worthy of scorn and laughter if we attack a puerile or imaginary adversary.

"But the number of people incapable of appreciating the true color of things is not limited to those who enshroud them in black.

"There are others, on the contrary, who obstinately insist upon surrounding them with a halo of sunlight only existing in their imagination.

"For such deluded people, obstacles seen from a distance take on the most attractive appearance; they would be readily disposed to enjoy them and only consent to allow them a certain importance if they absolutely obstruct the way.

"But until the moment when impossibility confronts them, do they deny its existence or underrate its importance by attributing a favorable influence to it.

"This propensity to see all in the ideal would be enviable if it did not wound common sense, which revenges itself by refusing to these improvident people the help of the reasoning power necessary to sustain them in the crisis of discouragement which brings about irresistibly the establishment of error.

"These unbalanced people rarely experience success, for they are unable, as long as their blindness lasts, to mark out a line of serious conduct for themselves.

"All projects built on the quicksand of false deductions will perish without even leaving behind them material sufficient to reconstruct them.

"It is impossible to combat strongly enough this tendency to self-delusion, which inclines us to become the prey of untruth, by preventing the birth of faith, based on preceding success.

"Sincere conviction, on the contrary, will lead us to refute strongly all the false arguments, which impede thought and would choke it in order to allow unadulterated pleasure to be installed on the ruins of common sense.

"The battle of life demands warriors and conquerors as well as critics, less brilliant, perhaps, but just as worthy of admiration, for their mission is equally important, although infinitely more obscure.

"Whether they are peasants tilling the field or rich capitalists manipulating their gold, those who work in order to satisfy the needs or luxury of this existence are fighters whose hours are spent in occupations more or less dangerous.

"From time to time, however, a cessation of hostilities is produced; such always follows the appearance of common sense which, by giving to things their true proportions, causes the greater part of inequalities to disappear.

"Finally, those who cultivate this virtue unostentatiously will always be protected from the caprices of fortune; if they are poor, common sense will indicate to them the way to cease to be poor, and, if chance has given them birth in opulence, the counsels of experience will demonstrate to them the frailty of possessions that one has not acquired by personal effort."

This conclusion is strikingly true, for it is certain that prosperity attained by personal effort is less likely to fade away than an inherited fortune, whose owner can only understand the ordinary pleasure of a possession which he has not ardently desired.

They who are the makers of their own position are more able to maintain it; they know the price of the efforts which had to be make in order to construct it, and, armed with common sense, they are as able to defend their treasure as to enjoy the sweet savor of a thing which they have desired, longed for, and won by the force of their will and judgment, placed at the service of circumstances and directed toward success.

Lesson XI

Common Sense and Self-Control

"Where life manifests itself," says Yoritomo, "antagonism always springs up.

"In the eternal struggle between the individual and social soul, each of which, in its turn, is victorious or vanquished, a truce is declared only if self-control is allied to common sense, in order to maintain the equilibrium between individual sentiment, natural to each one of us, and the ideas of humankind as a whole.

"All classes of society are subject to this law, and, from the proudest prince to the humblest peasant, every one is obliged to harmonize their social duties with their personal obligations.

"Those who understand how to imbibe thoroughly the lessons of common sense, never ignore the fact that morality is always closely related to self-interest.

"If each one of us would observe this rule individual happiness would not be long in creating a harmony from which all people would benefit.

"One thing we should avoid, for the attainment of universal tranquility, is the perpetual conflict between individual and social interest.

"The day when each one of us can comprehend that we are a part of this 'all,' which is called society; we will admit that sinning against society may be considered the same as sinning against oneself.

"Passing one day before an immense cabin, built of bamboo, which stood near a rice plantation, I perceived a man who hid himself from my view, without however being able to escape my notice altogether. I went resolutely to him, to ask him the explanation of his suspicious movement.

"After an unsuccessful attempt to escape, he resigned himself to allow me to approach him, and I understood the reason of his apprehension.

"He was carrying several pieces of bamboo which he had detached from the house. He wanted, he said, to make a little blaze because the dampness was chilling him.

"Without replying to him, I led him by the hand to the place where the branches taken away had left a large space, a kind of opening in the side of the house, through which a keen wind was rushing.

"'Look,' I said to him, 'the blaze that you are going to make will warm you for a few minutes, but, during the whole night the cold wind will freeze you and your companions.

"'In order to procure for yourself an agreeable but passing sensation you are going to inflict upon them continued sufferings, of which you can not escape your share.'

"The man hung his head and said: 'I had not thought of this; I was cold and I allowed myself to be tempted by the anticipated pleasure of warming myself, even if only for a few minutes.'

"And, convinced by common sense, he repaired the harm which he had done, first by reason of selfishness, then by thoughtlessness, but, above all, by lack of self-control.

"To dominate oneself to the point of not allowing oneself to become the slave of miserable contingencies which appear as temptations to self-indulgence, and conceal from their pettiness the beauty of the consistent action—this is only given to the chosen few and can only be understood by those who cultivate common sense."

Is this to say that reasoning should be a school for abnegation?

Such a thought is far from our minds.

Neither habitual abnegation nor modesty is among the militant virtues, nor for this reason ought the critics often relegate them to their proper place, which is the last, very close to defects to which they closely approach and among whose ranks one must sometimes go in order to discover them.

But, apart from the question of a sterile abnegation, we must foresee that it may be important not to overestimate one's individual interests, to the visible detriment of the general interest.

This is a fault common to all those who have not been initiated into the practice of self-control by means of reasoning based on solid premises.

They are ready to sacrifice very great interests, which do not seem to concern them directly, for some immediate paltry gratification.

"They act," said the philosopher, "like a peasant who should risk his harvest in order to avoid paying the prince the rent which belongs to him.

"Common sense teaches us that we should call to our assistance self-control, in order to repress the tendencies which tempt us to sacrifice the general interest to some personal and vehement desire.

"Rarely do we find our advantage in separating ourselves from the mass, and the prosperity of the greatest number is always the cradle of individual fortunes."

Leaving questions of primary importance to come to the subtleties of detail in which he delights, Yoritomo speaks to us of self-control allied to common sense, extolling to us its good effects in practical questions of our every-day life.

"We too often confound," said he, "self-control and liberty.

"We are tempted to believe that a slave cannot possess it, inasmuch as it is the special possession of all those to whom riches give a superior position in the world.

"How profound is this error!

"The lowest slave can enjoy this liberty, which is worth all others: self-control, which confers intellectual independence more precious than the most precious of possessions, whereas the most powerful prince may be altogether ignorant of this blessing.

"There are dependent souls who, for want of the necessary strength to escape from vassalage to the external impressions will always drag on, feeble and oppressed by the exactions of a mental servitude from which they can not free themselves.

"Others rise proudly, ready to command circumstances, which they dominate with all the power of their volition governed by reason.

"It is common sense which will guide them in this ascent by keeping them within the limits assigned to those things pertaining to reason and rectitude of mind.

"Before everything, it is well not to forget that this faculty invites those who cultivate it to seek always for exact facts.

"Knowledge, in all its aspects is, then, a perfect educator for those who do not wish to build on the flimsy foundation of approximate truth.

"In pronouncing the word knowledge, we do not wish to speak of abstract studies which are only accessible to a small number; we wish to express the thought of instruction embracing all things, even the most humble and ordinary.

"A man from the city was walking in the country one day, not far from a vast swamp.

"All around it were a few miserable huts, the shelter of some peasants whose business it was to gather the reeds from the borders, weaving them into large baskets to be sold afterward in the neighboring country.

"Little by little twilight descended, slowly enveloping all things in a mist of ashy gray, and vapors arose from afar over the stagnant water.

"The man from the city trembled, believing that he recognized phantoms in this moving vapor; he sought to flee, but, unfamiliar with the locality, he ran along the side of the swamp without finding the end of it.

"Exhausted from fatigue and trembling with fear, he resolved to knock at one of the cabins.

"He was welcomed by a basket-maker, to whom he related his fright, adding that he was unable to understand how this man found the courage to live in a place haunted in such a terrible way.

"The peasant smiled and explained to the man, whose intellectual culture was, however, infinitely superior to his own, by what phenomenon of evaporation these mirages were produced.

"He demonstrated to him that these phantoms were only harmless vapors, and the city man admired the knowledge which common sense had taught the ignorant one."

And Yoritomo concluded:

"This peasant gave there a proof of what self-control allied to common sense can do.

"Instead of allowing himself to be influenced by appearances, he confined himself to reflection, and observation aided by attention led him to a deduction resting on truth.

"The essential factor of control is cool-headedness, which permits of seeing things in their true light, and forbids us to gild them or to darken them, according to our state of mind at the time."

The Shogun adds:

"Fear, hideous fear, is a sentiment unknown to those whose soul communes with self-control and common sense.

"The first of these qualities will produce a fiat resolution tending to calmness, at the same time that it makes a powerful appeal to cool-headedness, which permits of reflection.

"Fear is always the confession of a weakness which disavows struggle and wishes to ignore the name of adversary.

"Cool-headedness is the evanescent examination of forces, either physical or intellectual, with reference to supposed danger.

"Without self-control cool-headedness cannot exist; but it only develops completely under the influence of common sense that dictates to it the reasons for its existence.

"Cool-headedness, by leaving us our liberty of thought, enlightens us undoubtedly on the nature of danger, at the same time that it suggests to us the way to avoid it, if it really exists.

"There can not be a question of fear for those who possess the faculties of which we have just spoken, for it is well known that, from the moment when the cause of fear is defined it ceases to exist; it becomes stupid illusion or a real enemy.

"In the one case, as in the other, it ought not to excite anxiety any longer, but contempt or the desire to fight it.

"For those whose mind is not yet strong enough to resolve on one or other of these decisions it will be well to take up again the argument indicated in the preceding pages, and to say:

"Either the object of my fear really exists, and, in this ease, I must determine its nature exactly, in order to use the proper means first to combat it and then to conquer it.

"Or it is only an illusion, and I am going to seek actively for that which produces it, in order never again to fall into the error of which my senses have just been the dupes."

Looking over these manuscripts, so rich in valuable advice, we find once more the following lines:

"Self-control and cool-headedness are above all necessary to aid in dissimulating impressions.

"It is very bad to allow one of the speakers in a dialog to read the mind of those who speaks to him or her like an open book.

"Those whose thoughts are impressed vividly on the surface is always placed at a glaring disadvantage.

"The thought of glorifying hypocrisy is far from our minds, for it has nothing to do with the attitude which we recommend.

"Hypocrites strive to assume emotions which they do not feel.

"People gifted with cool-headedness are intent on never allowing them to be seen.

"It keeps their adversaries in ignorance of the effect produced by their reasoning and allows him them to take their chance, until the moment when, in spite of this feigned indifference, they reveal themselves and permits their mind to be seen.

"Now, to know the designs of rivals, when they are ignorant of those that we have conceived, is one of the essential factors of success.

"In every way, those who are informed about the projects of their adversaries walks preceded by a torch of light, while the adversaries, if they can not divine their opponent's plans, continue to fight in darkness."

The most elementary common sense counsels then cool-headedness when exchanging ideas, even when the discussion is of quite an amicable nature.

From this habit there will result a very praiseworthy propensity to exercise self-control, which is only a sort of superior cool-headedness.

It is also the cause of a noble pride, because it is more difficult to win a victory over one's passions than to conquer ordinary enemies, and those who, with the support of common sense, succeed in ruling themselves, can calculate, without arrogance, the hour when they will reign over the minds of others.

Lesson XII

Common Sense Does Not Exclude Great Aspirations

"A very common error," says Yoritomo "is that which consists in classifying common sense among the amorphous virtues, and only applicable to things and to people whose fundamental principle is materiality. This is a calumny that is spread broadcast by fools who scatter their lives to the four winds of caprice and extravagance.

"Not only does common sense not exclude beauty, but it really aids in its inception and protects its growth by maintaining the reasons which produced its appearance.

"Without it, the reign of the most admired things would be of short duration, granting that the want of logic had not prevented their production.

"What is there more commendable than the love of work, devotion to science, ambition to succeed?

"Could all this exist if common sense did not intervene to permit the development of the deductions on which are based the resolutions that inspired in us these aspirations.

"But this is not all; without logic, which permits us to give them solidity, the most serious resolutions would soon become nothing but vague projects, shattered as soon as formed.

"In common sense lies the cause and the object of things.

"It is common sense which makes us realize that difference that few persons are willing to analyze, and which lies between judgment and opinion.

"We almost always succeed in readily confounding them, and from this mistake results a too frequent cause of failures.

"Opinion is a conviction which is capable of modification.

"In addition to this, as it is based on mere indications and probability, it is rarely free from the personal element.

"Opinion depends upon the favorite inclination, upon the mood of the moment, upon sundry considerations, which direct it almost always toward the desired solution.

"Also it depends often on thoughtfulness or on the inexactness of the initial representation, which we are pleased to disguise slightly at first, then little by little to color in accordance with our desires.

"Falsehood does not necessarily enter into this process of tricking things out; it is three-quarters of the time, the result of an illusion which we are prone to perpetuate within us.

"We are too often in the position of the three wise men who, while rummaging in an old sarcophagus, discovered a vase whose primitive function they were unable to determine with any certainty.

"One of them was a poet and an idealist.

"The second only prized positive things.

"The third belonged to the category of melancholy people.

"After a few days devoted to special research work, they met together again in order to communicate to each other their different opinions about the exhumed vase.

"'I have found the secret,' said the first.

"'I also,' affirmed the second.

"'I also have found it,' replied the third.

"And each one based his opinion on preconceived notions which reflected their bent of mind:

"'This vase,' said the first, 'was intended to hold incense, which they burned in that epoch, in the belief that the smoke dispelled the evil spirits.'

"'Nonsense!' cried out the second; 'this vase is a pot which at that time served as a receptacle for keeping spices.'

"'Not so!' insisted the third, 'it is an urn of antiquated design used for receiving tears; that is all.'

"These three serious men were certainly sincere in giving explanations which each one of them declared decisive. They expressed opinions which they believed implicitly and which their respective natures directed irresistibly toward their peculiar bents of mind.

"Judgment, in order to be free from all which is not common sense, ought then to put aside all personal predilections, all desire to form a conclusion to humor our inclinations.

"Absolute impartiality of judgment is one of the rarest gifts and at the same time is the noblest quality which we can possess."

We should then conclude, with the Shogun, that common sense aids in the production of noble aspirations, and is not concerned only with that which relates to materiality, as so many people would have us understand.

The Nippon philosopher teaches us also the part that he assigns to the habitual practice of goodness.

"We are too easily persuaded," he says, "that goodness, like beauty, is a gift of birth.

"It is time to destroy an error rooted in our minds for too many centuries.

"Goodness is acquired by reasoning and logic, as are so many other qualities and it is common sense that governs its formation.

"Have we ever reflected over the sum total of annoyances that people, who are essentially wicked, add every day to those imposed upon them by circumstances?

"Are we capable of appreciating the joys of life when impatience makes the nerves vibrate or when anger brandishes its torch in the bends and turns of the brain?

"People who lack goodness are the first to be punished for their defect. Serenity is unknown to them and they live in perpetual agitation, caused by the irritation which they experience on the slightest provocation."

Common sense indicates then in an irrefutable way that there is every advantage in being good.

Yoritomo proves it to us, by using his favorite syllogism:

"Happiness," he says, "is above all a combination of harmony and absence of sorrow.

"Wickedness, by inspiring us with discontent and anger, disturbs this harmony.

"We must, therefore, banish wickedness, that we may cultivate goodness, which is the creator of harmony."

Continuing still further the same argument, he adds:

"Common sense would have the tendency even to make us promise to be good, so as to satisfy our own egotism.

Goodness creates smiles; to sow happiness around one, is a way of having neither eyes nor heart offended by the sight of people in tears; it is the eliciting of an agreeable joy, whose rays will shed a golden light over our life; is it not more pleasing to hear the ring of laughter than to listen to painful sobs?"

So, we should never lose an opportunity of being good and that without mental reservation.

Gratitude is not the possession of every soul and those who do good may expect to receive ingratitude.

They will not suffer from it, if they have done good, not in the way creditors do who intend to come on the very day appointed to claim a debt, but as givers who fulfill their mission from which they are expecting a personal satisfaction, without thinking of any acknowledgment for what they have done.

If the debtor is filled with gratitude, the joy of being good is that much increased.

There is a species of common sense of a particularly noble quality that is called moral sense and which the Shogun defines thus:

"The moral sense is the common sense of the soul; it is the superior power of reasoning which stands before us that we may be prevented from passively following our instincts; it is by its assistance that we succeed without too much difficulty in climbing the steep paths of duty.

"This sense discerns an important quality, which puts us on our guard against the danger of certain theories, whose brilliancy might seduce us.

"It is the moral sense which indicates to us the point of delimitation separating legitimate concessions from forbidden license.

"It allows us to go as far as the dangerous place where the understanding with conscience might become compromised and, by reasoning, proves to us that there would be serious danger in proceeding further.

"It is the moral sense which distinguishes civilized people from brutes; it is the regulator of the movements of the soul and the faithful indicator of the actions which depend on it."

We must really pity those who are deprived of moral sense for they are the prey of all the impulses created in them by the brute nature, which sleeps in the depths of each human creature.

Those people whose moral sense is developed will live at peace with themselves, for they will only know the evil of doubt when they realize the satisfaction of having conquered it.

Moral sense, like common sense, is formed by reasoning and is fostered by the practice of constant application.

It is the property of those who avoid evil, as others avoid the spatter of mud, through horror of the stains that result from it.

Those who do not have this apprehension flounder about, cover themselves with mud, sink in it and finally are swallowed up.

Yoritomo again takes up the defense of common sense, with reference to the arts.

"Can one imagine," he says, "a painter conceiving a picture and grouping his figures in such a way as to violate the rules of common sense?

"We should be doomed, if this were true, to see men as tall as oak-trees and houses resembling children's toy constructions, placed without reference to equilibrium among green or pink animals, whose legs had queer shapes.

"Psychotic individuals may represent nature thus, which seems to them outlined in strange forms.

"But people of common sense reproduce things just as sound judgment conceives of them; if they throw around them at times the halo of beauty which seems exaggerated, let us not decry them.

"Beauty exists everywhere; it dwells in the most humble objects, makes all around us resplendent and, if we refuse to see it, we are blinded by an unjust prejudice, or our minds are not open to the faculty of contemplation.

"It is revealed above all to those who cultivate common sense and reject the sophistries of untruth that they may surround themselves with truth.

"Such people scorn trivial casualties; they adopt an immutable rule, reasoning, which permits them to deduce, to judge, and afterward to produce.

"All beautiful creations are derived from this source.

"The most admirable inventions would never have been known if common sense had not helped them to be produced, strengthening those who conceived them by the support of logic, which demonstrated to them the truth of their presumptions.

"Authority follows, based on the experience which, by maintaining the effect of judgment, has armed them with the strength of the mind, the true glory of peaceful conquerors."

Would one not say that the Shogun, in writing these lines, foresaw the magnificent efforts which we are witnessing each day and that from the depths of time he caught a glimpse of these brave conquerors of the air and of space, whose great deeds, seeming at times the result of a crazy temerity, are in reality only homage rendered to common sense, which has permitted them to calculate the value of their initiative without mistake?

And one cannot be denied the pleasure of entering once more into close communion of thought with the old philosopher when he says:

"Enthusiasm is of crystal but common sense is of brass."

www.ingramcontent.com/pod-product-compliance
Lightning Source LLC
Chambersburg PA
CBHW071226080526
44587CB00013BA/1519